Nadsokor

★Jalor

Vilmir

Uhas y

Vilmiro

THE OLDEST
OCEAN

STRAITS OF
VILMIR

ISLE OF
PURPLE
TOWNS

Cadsandria

Ramasaz

Tarkesh

★Raschil

Sequaloris

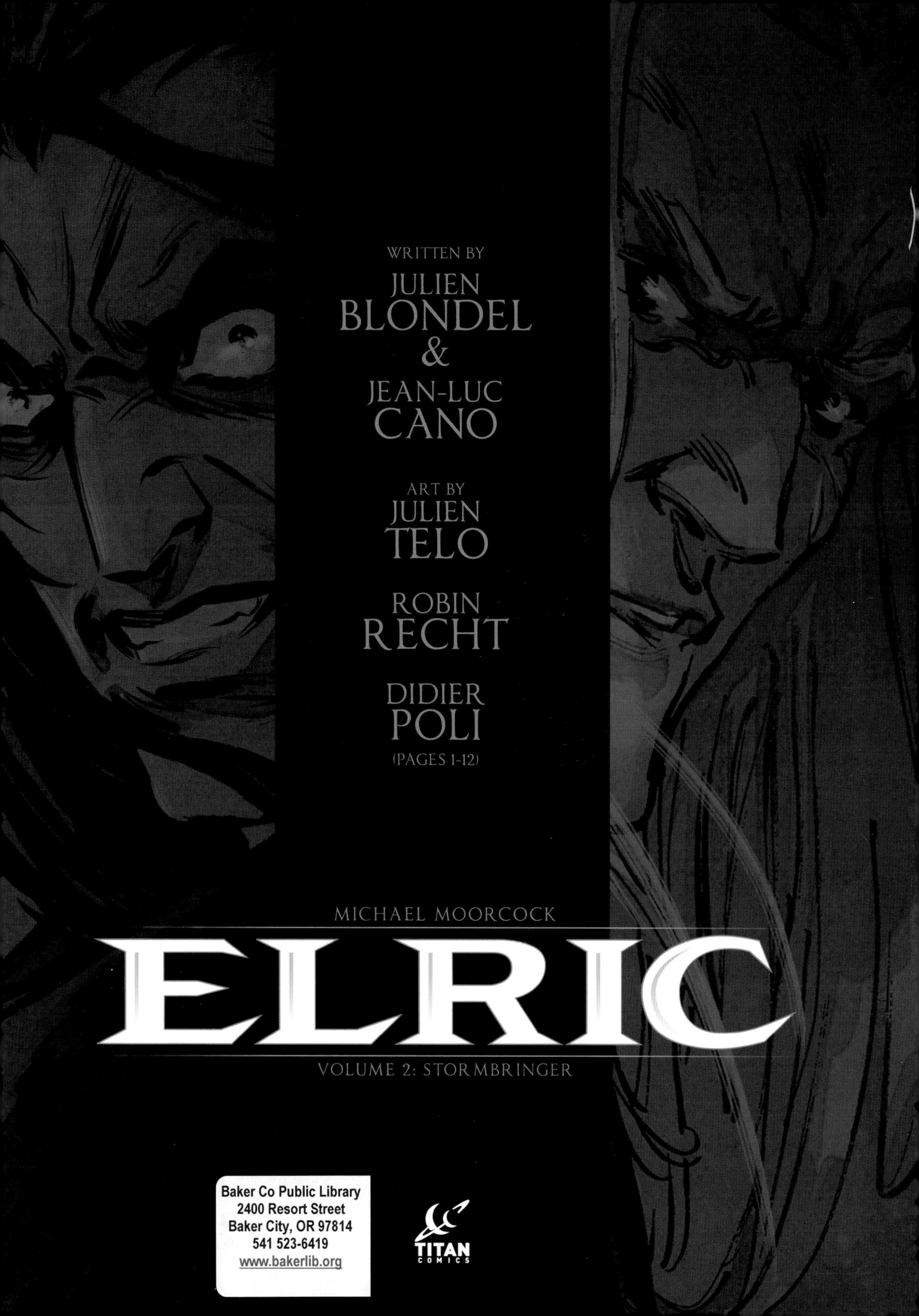

WRITTEN BY

JULIEN
BLONDEL
&
JEAN-LUC
CANO

ART BY

JULIEN
TELO

ROBIN
RECHT

DIDIER
POLI
(PAGES 1-12)

MICHAEL MOORCOCK

ELRIC

VOLUME 2: STORMBRINGER

TITAN COMICS

MICHAEL MOORCOCK

ELRIC

VOLUME 2: STORMBRINGER

WRITTEN BY
JULIEN BLONDEL & JEAN-LUC CANO

BASED ON THE NOVEL BY
MICHAEL MOORCOCK

ART BY
JULIEN TELO, ROBIN RECHT, DIDIER POLI (Pages 1-12)

COLORS BY
ROBIN RECHT, JEAN BASTIDE & SCARLETT SMULKOWSKI

COVER ART
JEAN BASTIDE & ROBIN RECHT

TRANSLATED BY
EDWARD GAUVIN

LETTERING BY
GABRIELA HOUSTON

Elric Volume 2: Stormbringer
ISBN: 9781782761259

Published by Titan Comics
A division of Titan Publishing Group Ltd.
144 Southwark Street. London SE1 0UP

A CIP catalogue record for this title is available from the British Library.
First edition: May 2015
Originally published in 2014 by Éditions Glénat, France as Elric: Stormbringer

10 9 8 7 6 5 4 3 2 1

Printed in China.
Titan Comics. TC0200

ELRIC
VOLUME 2: STORMBRINGER

Collection Editor
Lizzie Kaye

Collection Designer
Dan Bura

Senior Editor
Steve White

Titan Comics Editorial
Andrew James, Tom Williams, Kirsten Murrey

Production Manager
Obi Onuora

Production Supervisor
Maria Pearson, Jackie Flook

Production Assistant
Peter James

Art Director
Oz Browne

Studio Manager
Emma Smith

Circulation Manager
Steve Tothill

Marketing Manager
Ricky Claydon

Senior Marketing and Press Executive
Owen Johnson

Publishing Manager
Darryl Tothill

Publishing Director
Chris Teather

Operations Director
Leigh Baulch

Executive Director
Vivian Cheung

Publisher
Nick Landau

ACKNOWLEDGEMENTS

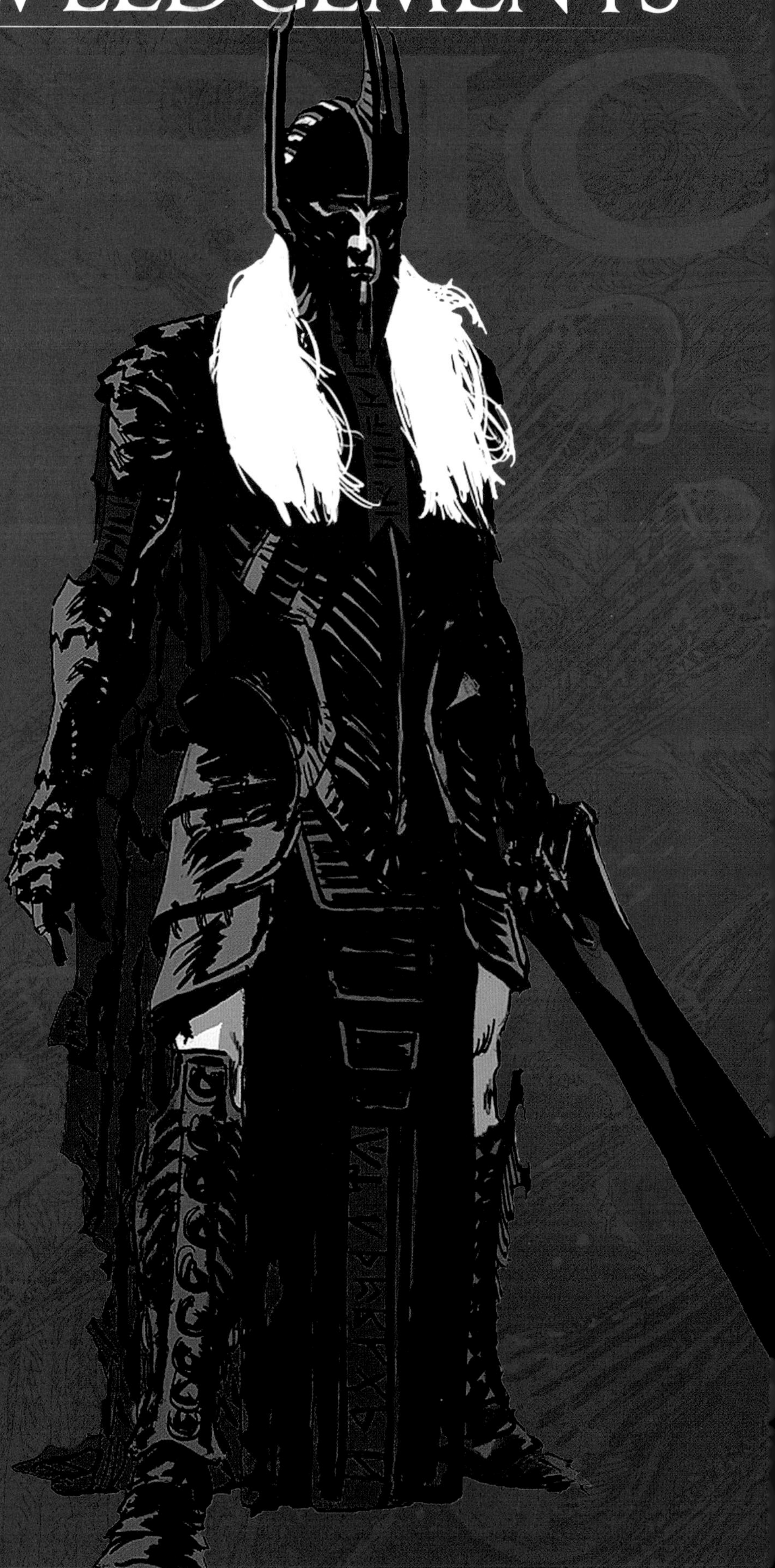

Warm thanks from the authors to Mathieu Lauffray for his help with the pencils on pages 35, 36, and 37. Jean Bastide for his help with the pencils on pages 38 and 39 and Jean-Baptiste Hostache for his help with the backgrounds on page 43.

Thanks to:
Scarlett, Jean-Luc, and Julien, who joined us aboard the Ship of Destiny, and to my she-wolf, who let me join her on hers.

Julien Blondel

Thanks to:
Julien Blondel, my brother-in-arms, eternal thanks for inviting me along on this incredible adventure. Benoît Cousin, for his patience, kindness, and precious confidence in this, my first collaboration. Robin Recht, for his incredible talent, his extraordinary personality, and his friendship and finally, Nicolas Martin, who one fine day in 1992, in the middle-school courtyard, introduced me to Elric of Melniboné and Stormbringer. Wherever you are today, you have all of my affection.

Jean-Luc Cano

Thanks to the entire team for welcoming me aboard this grand adventure, and for believing in me. Thanks to my loved ones for their daily support.

Julien Telo

Huge thanks to Mr Moorcock.

Robin Recht

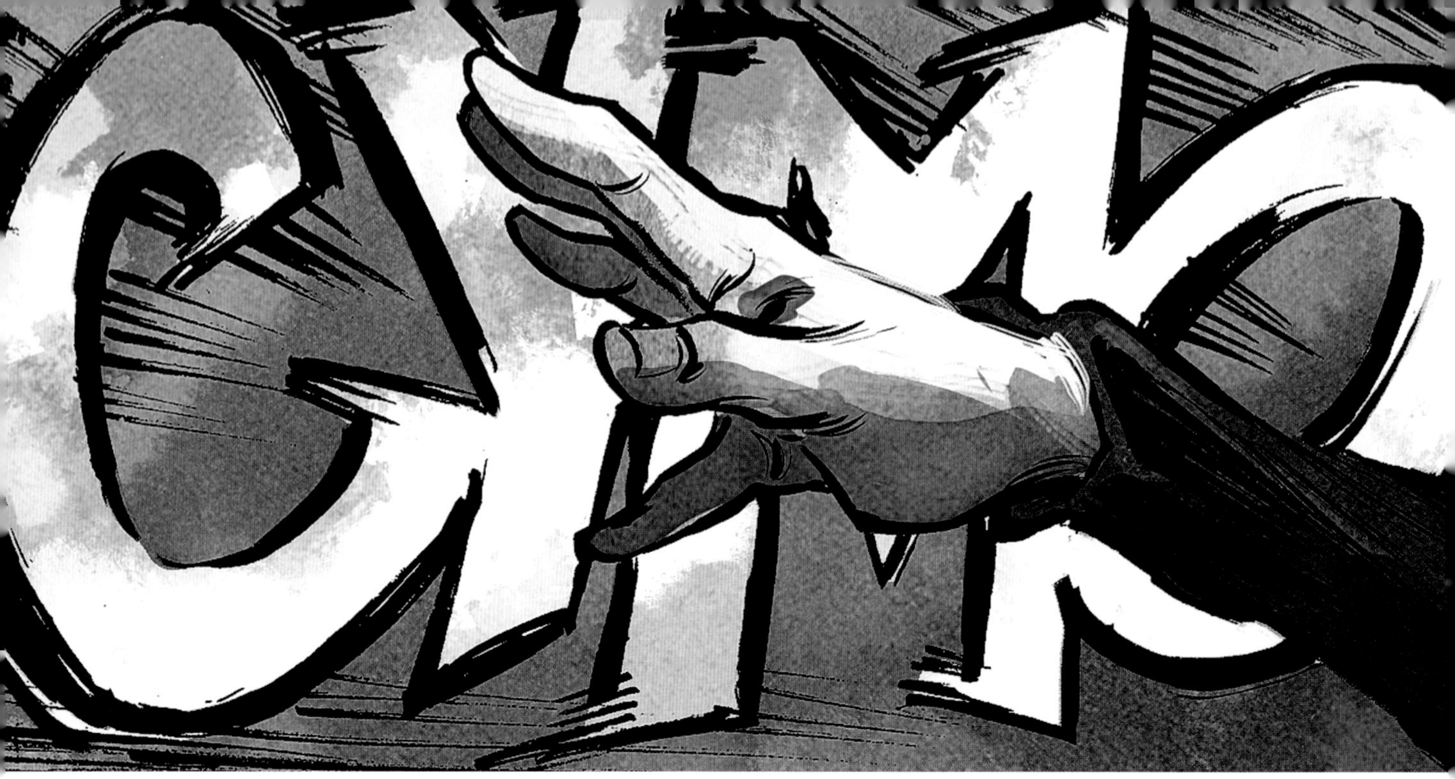

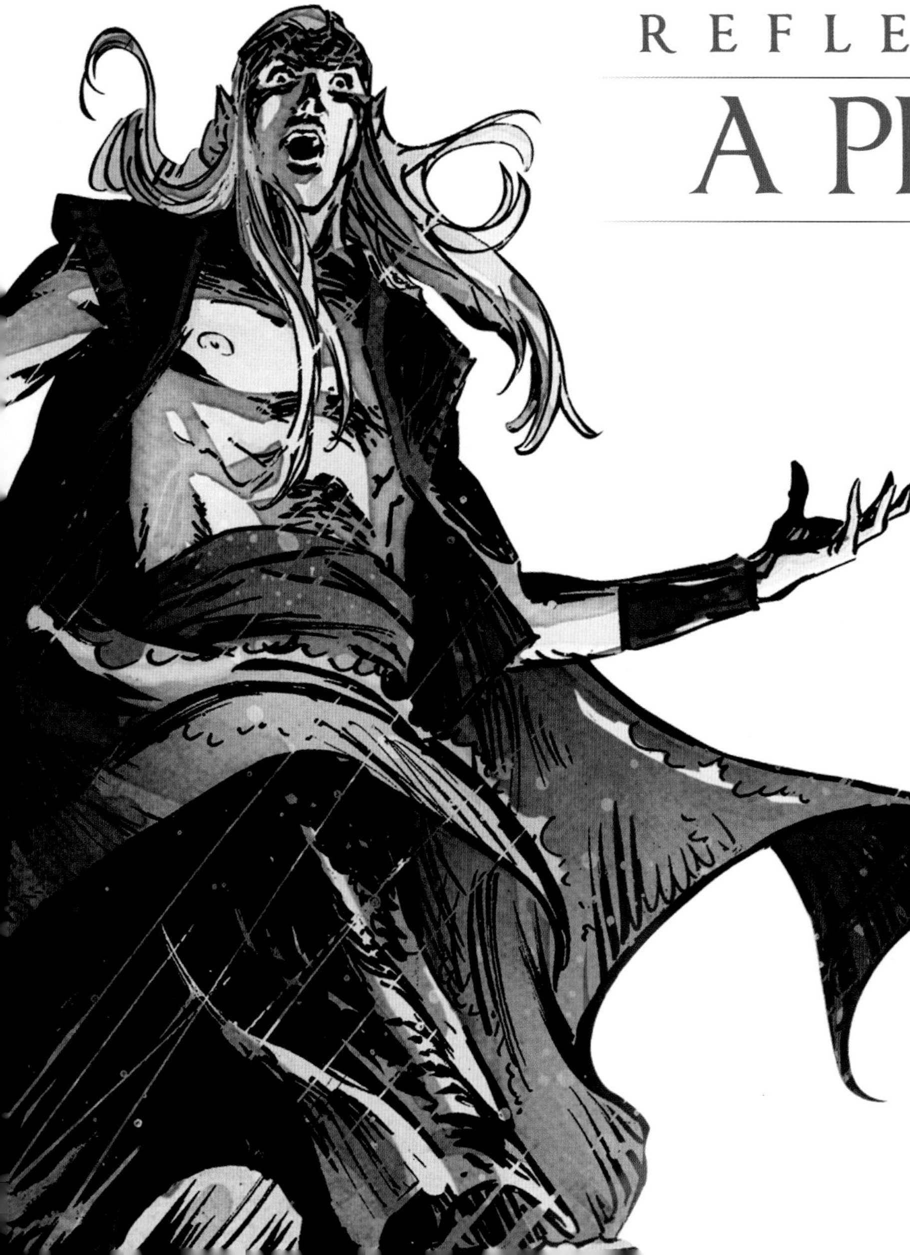

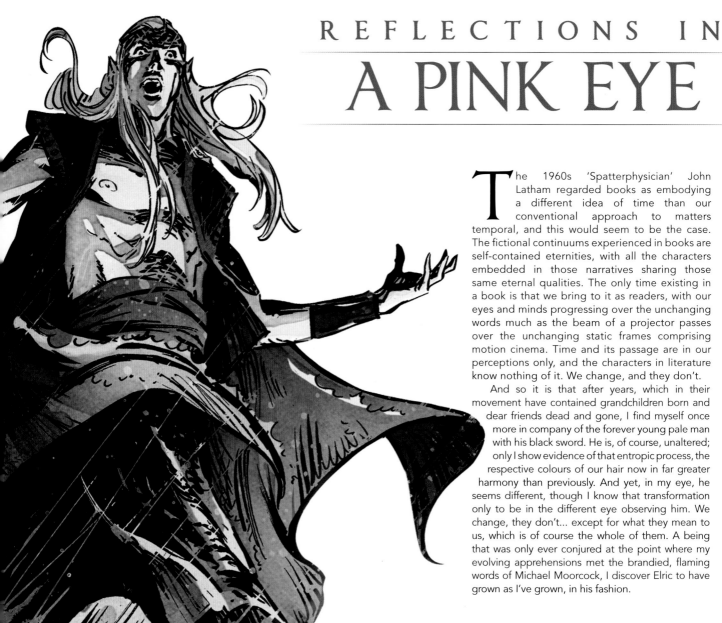

REFLECTIONS IN A PINK EYE

The 1960s 'Spatterphysician' John Latham regarded books as embodying a different idea of time than our conventional approach to matters temporal, and this would seem to be the case. The fictional continuums experienced in books are self-contained eternities, with all the characters embedded in those narratives sharing those same eternal qualities. The only time existing in a book is that we bring to it as readers, with our eyes and minds progressing over the unchanging words much as the beam of a projector passes over the unchanging static frames comprising motion cinema. Time and its passage are in our perceptions only, and the characters in literature know nothing of it. We change, and they don't.

And so it is that after years, which in their movement have contained grandchildren born and dear friends dead and gone, I find myself once more in company of the forever young pale man with his black sword. He is, of course, unaltered; only I show evidence of that entropic process, the respective colours of our hair now in far greater harmony than previously. And yet, in my eye, he seems different, though I know that transformation only to be in the different eye observing him. We change, they don't... except for what they mean to us, which is of course the whole of them. A being that was only ever conjured at the point where my evolving apprehensions met the brandied, flaming words of Michael Moorcock, I discover Elric to have grown as I've grown, in his fashion.

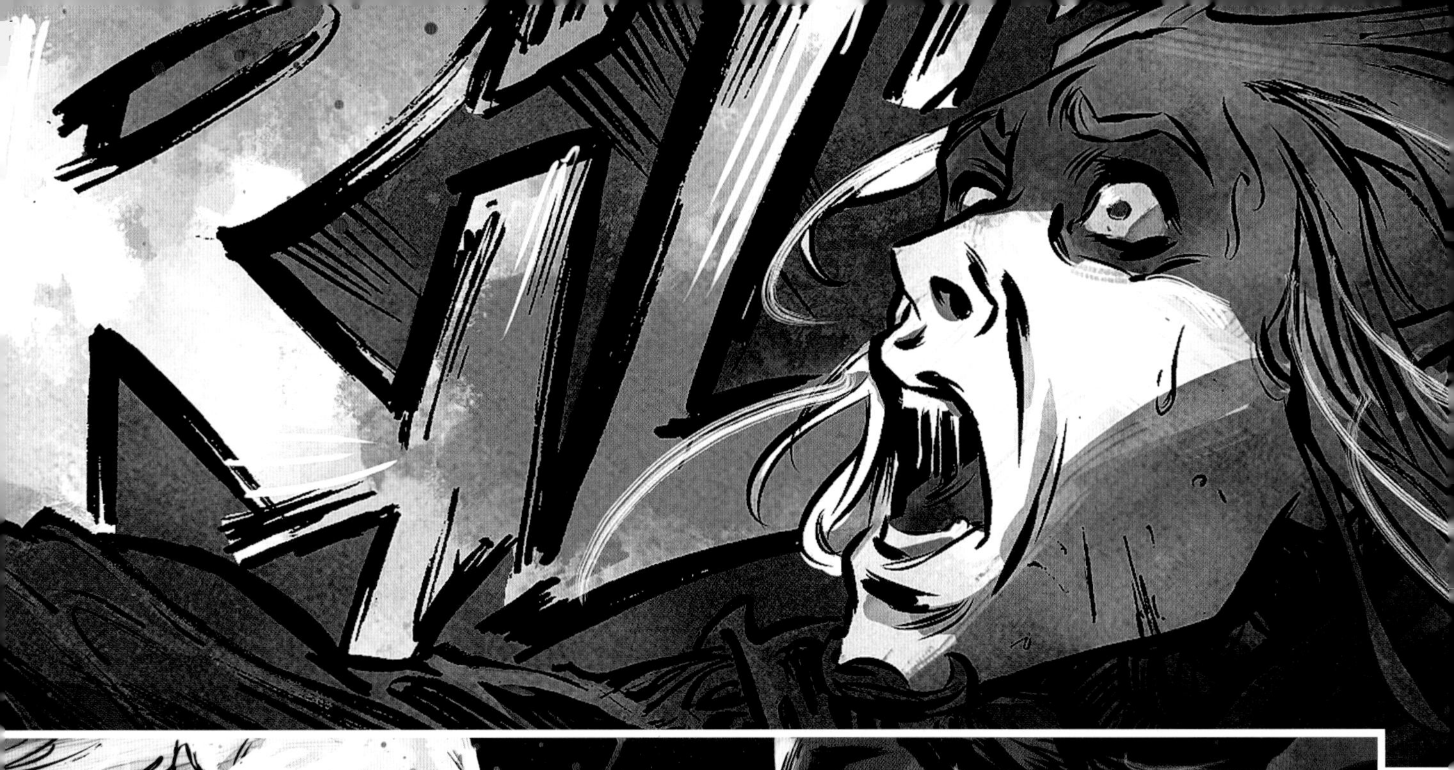

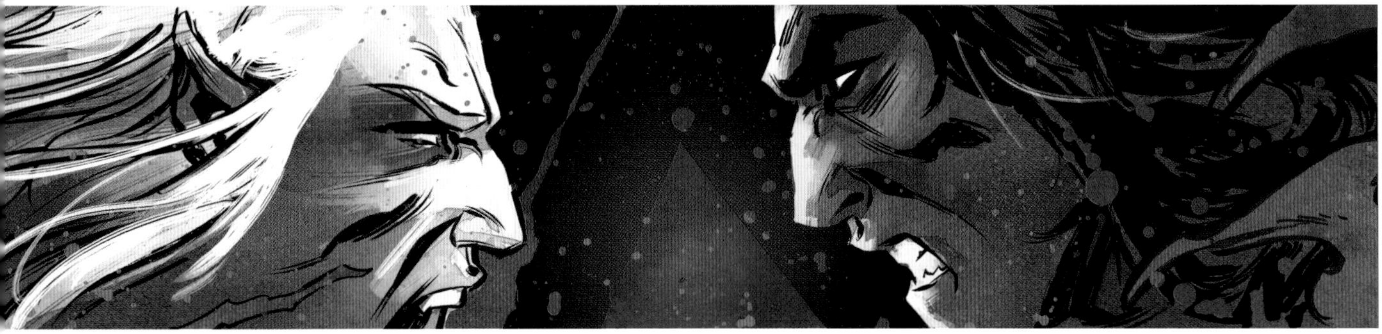

...it's not difficult to see a dissolute and mournful echo of the cursed aristocrat albino in the postures struck by David Bowie and his darkly glamorous contemporaries.

Alan Moore

At fourteen years old, the imagined doomed lord of Melniboné that I was capable of comprehending was assembled wholly from fourteen-year-old preoccupations which, in the explosive middle-sixties, seemed pandemic throughout Western culture. The prevailing sense of individual alienation and estrangement from the processes of regular society, whether occasioned by an ordinary adolescence or across a population by the agency of two world wars and an alarmingly accelerated modern pace of life, was perfectly personified in that bleached skin from which the reassuring hues of a Dickensian past had bled away, in serum-coloured eyes, and in that monstrous and empowering blackness on which we'd become dependent. This, in retrospect, was a blackness of Empire.

That disorienting funhouse period and its apparent simultaneous advent of both personal and cultural puberty surged, both inside and out, with the ferocious Shiva-energies of intertwined creation and destruction. An angst-ridden teenager filled with impatient urges to create was made aware of the dead hand of educational, parental or otherwise generational authority that rested heavily on their ambitions from above. Similarly, the post-war world which shaped both Moorcock and myself was bursting with new culture and ideas, yet found itself restrained beneath the attitudes and galvanised reflexes of an Empire that had died a decade earlier but was still in denial of its putrid, obvious mortality. All of us felt at war with our own heritage. All of us launched our fleets, resplendent and baroque, with wind-filled sails and sinking hearts against the mother country, necessary traitors.

It was not only in the incoherent frenzy of the decade's battles that the pallid prince of ruins epitomised its angry, patricidal zeitgeist, but also in its peacock flourishes of sex and intellect and Fauvist beauty. In the chalk complexioned charismatic, dressed exquisitely, cerebral often to the point of his own detriment, infused with a decadent Aubrey Beardsley sexuality, was a compelling icon perfectly tooled to the aspirations of its youthful writer, youthful audience and to those of the fledgling world-in-waiting springing up around them; the well-tailored, gorgeous tragedy we wished we were. At decade's end, with the hormonal pinball of both awkward individuals and the counter-culture which contained them hitting a long tail when faced with the dual disappointments of failed revolution and adulthood, it's not difficult to see a dissolute and mournful echo of the cursed aristocrat albino in the postures struck by David Bowie and his darkly glamorous contemporaries. Elric encapsulates those years, exotic and exhilarating and tormented, from their A-bomb shadowed beatnik genesis through to their jewelled and deliquescent aftermath, and on encountering him again I find that he has indeed changed, though only in so far as my views on that epoch and my own participation in its insurrections and its love-affairs has done so.

Looking at him now, the hollow alabaster cheeks and lupine eyes, each of us with our youthful wars behind us, I can view both Elric and my generation's florid affectations with affection, admiration even, rather than embarrassment. All parties had a lot to deal with and accomplished it in style, if not without a measure of catastrophe. We sacked the dreaming cities and read with alarm the manuals of our gods, discovering them to be filled with madness. We slew, unintentionally, the things we loved, wielding the black swords of our talent indiscriminately when the fever of revolt was on us, needing desperately the sustenance they fed us yet afraid of forfeiting our sanity, our souls. Both he and we confronted our collapsing empires and chaos-driven circumstances with considerable bravery, invention and a self-consuming passion; with our energetic madness and our lovely hair. He's aged well, in so far as he can be said to have aged at all.

There is, of course, the manner and the mode of this specific incarnation to consider. While by no means what you'd call a stranger to manifestations outside the prose medium for which he was created, Elric's forays into other media are still rare enough to warrant comment, and it must be said that it appears to be the comic field in which he has been made most welcome. This is perhaps unsurprising when one bears in mind that Michael Moorcock was himself apprenticed in the pictographic form during his teenage tenure on *Tarzan Adventures* with Sojan the Swordsman, Elric's substantially more conventional precursor. In fact, I am privately of the opinion than the rugged British picture-storytelling values that he will have unavoidably absorbed during those tender years have probably gone on to form the basis for the very visual dramatics that inform his work from *Stormbringer* to *Breakfast in the Ruins* to *Mother London*. Though this shaky thesis clearly needs more work, it cannot be denied that comics have consistently provided interesting soil for Moorcock's seminal ideas, whether that be in the Mal Dean and Glyn Jones-delineated comic strip adventures of Jerry Cornelius in underground tabloid *International Times* (*IT*) or in the somewhat de-fanged Marvel Comics adaptation of *Behold the Man* during the 1970s. But it has always been to Elric that the comics medium has made itself enduringly hospitable, with varying degrees of qualified success.

The work of Philippe Druillet, earliest among the runesword-bearer's illustrators to my knowledge, emphasised the scale and epic grandeur of the sinister Melnibonéan world while at the same

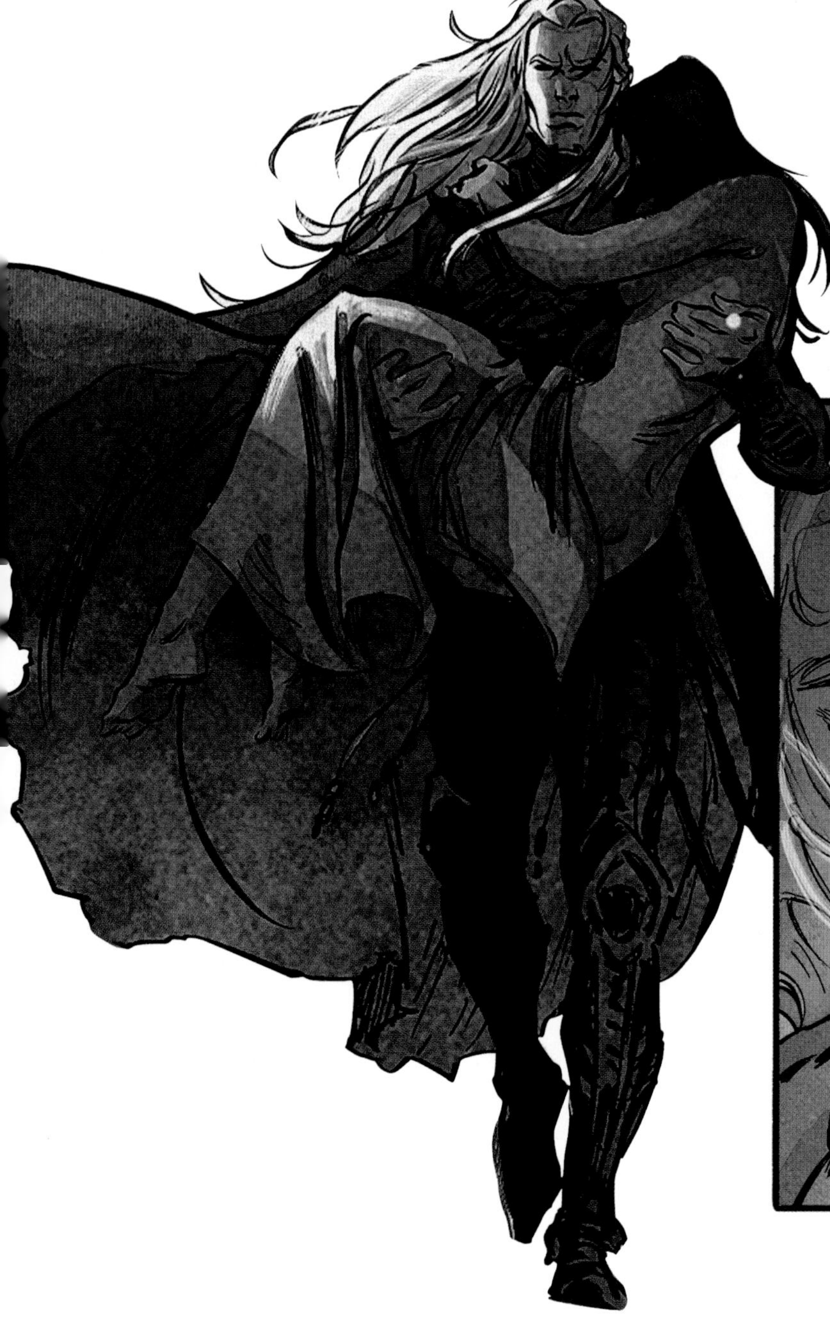

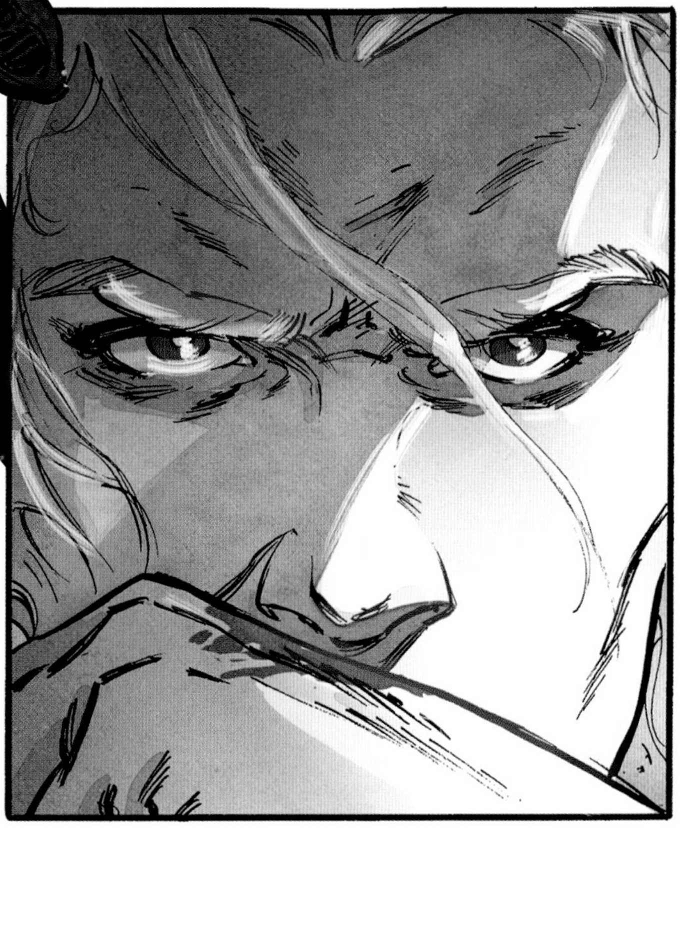

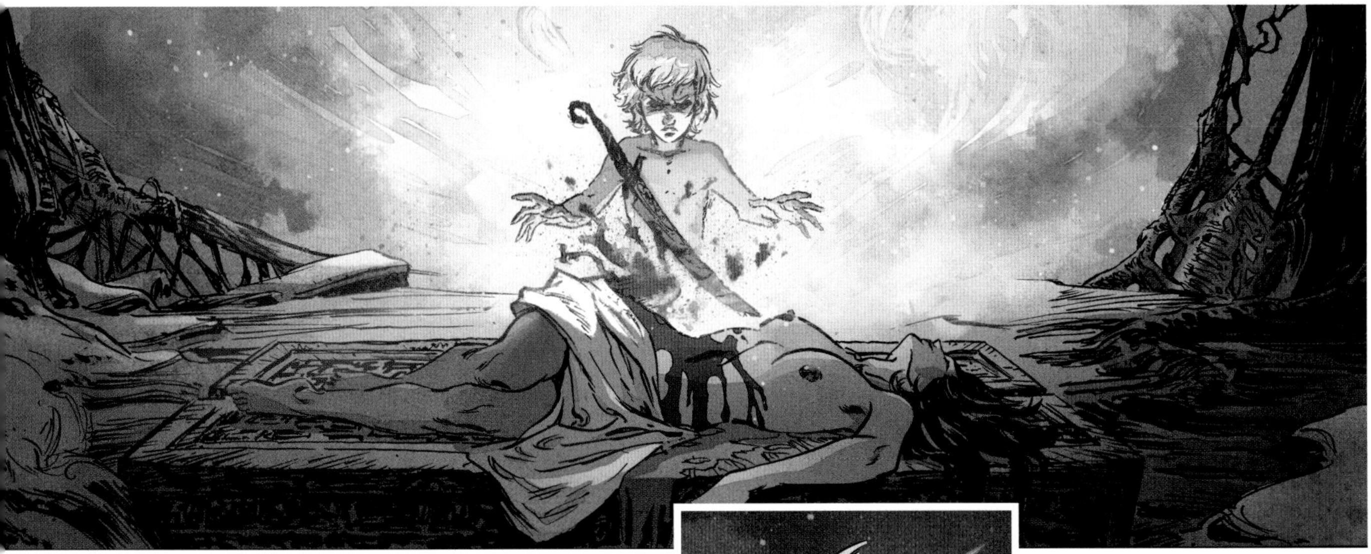

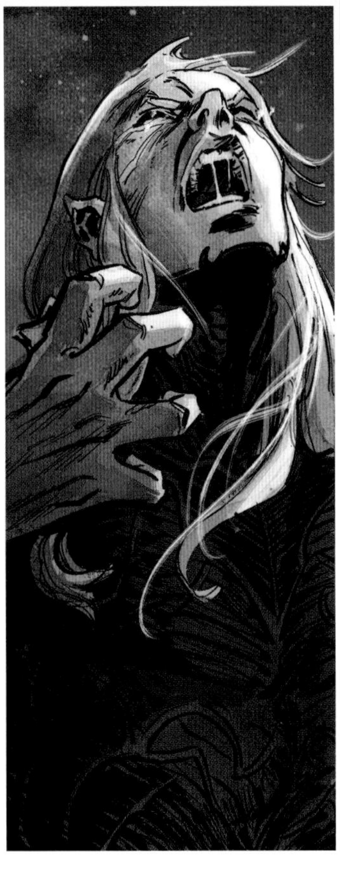

> I'd like to join with Moorcock in declaring this to be the most successful, true-in-spirit re-imagining of his fate-harrowed icon.
>
> **Alan Moore**

time lavishly indulging in the opportunities for decoration offered by that empire's fabled decadence. This latter obvious attraction of the Elric saga for an artist is also exemplified by the mid-eighties Michael Gilbert and Craig Russell adaptation of the character, beautifully rendered, lavishly ornate, but in my own opinion sharing the same problem that the Druillet work had evidenced, the emphasis on luscious imagery perhaps detracting from the pulp-paced dynamism of the plot and narrative. The white wolf's guest appearance in an early seventies edition of Marvel's Roy Thomas/Barry Smith-adapted *Conan* missed the mark even more widely (despite Smith's accomplished and Pre-Raphaelite stylings that one might have thought would be entirely suited to the task) thanks to the stark unsuitability of R.E. Howard's far less nuanced and unreconstructed sword-and-sorcery environment and Smith's unfortunate if well-intentioned borrowing of the strange pixie-hat adorning Jack Gaughn's U.S. paperback edition's cover illustration of the character.

Looking at this current offering, I can immediately see why Mike himself should claim this as his favourite Elric adaptation thus far. In the muscular and old-school comics storytelling that the skilled touch with design and decoration never overwhelms, I feel the massively accomplished illustrative spirit and inventiveness, if with a necessarily differing execution, of the marvellous Jim Cawthorne, the collaborator from whose heavily embellished correspondence with the writer Elric can be said to have emerged. It has a classic look, which in the world of comics is to say that it evokes the sturdy mix of functionality and elegance enjoyed by the most striking comic books of that most striking of decades, the nervous-wrecked, electrifying and progressive1950s.

Any new appearance by this odd and emblematic character who means so much to all of us (Elric, that is, not Moorcock, although...) is a cause for celebration, and especially when the author's artistic co-conspirators have clearly thought intensely about the original text-narrative adventures and their first creator's unimpeachable intentions and agendas. While I cannot readily imagine that amongst the deserved readership of this new presentation there'll be anyone discovering the blanched kin-slayer for the first time, if my prognosis should turn out to be not for the first time faulty and this is indeed the case, the newcomer to these pale, interesting, and yet far from anaemic exploits, while they'll doubtless go on to investigate the non-pictorial originals, should be assured that they have chanced upon one of those hens'-teeth adaptations that do not do a disservice to their murderous and haunted template. To the contrary, I'd like to join with Moorcock in declaring this to be the most successful, true-in-spirit re-imagining of his fate-harrowed icon. My congratulations to the talented creators, to Mike Moorcock, and to you, the reader, as you once again engage in your relationship with the forever young pale man and his black sword. You'll find him just as irresistible as ever.

Alan Moore,
Northampton, July 6th 2014.

Imrryr, the dreaming city, quakes in fear. Elric
of Melniboné, the white wolf, the philospher
emperor, has at last summoned the Lord of
Chaos, the great Arioch, to his aid.

Yet it is not for glory, nor vengeance, that
Elric calls on this arcane power... it is for
love. His queen, his life-source, the beautiful
Cymoril, has been taken by her traitorous
brother, Yyrkoon, and Elric will stop at
nothing to get her back...

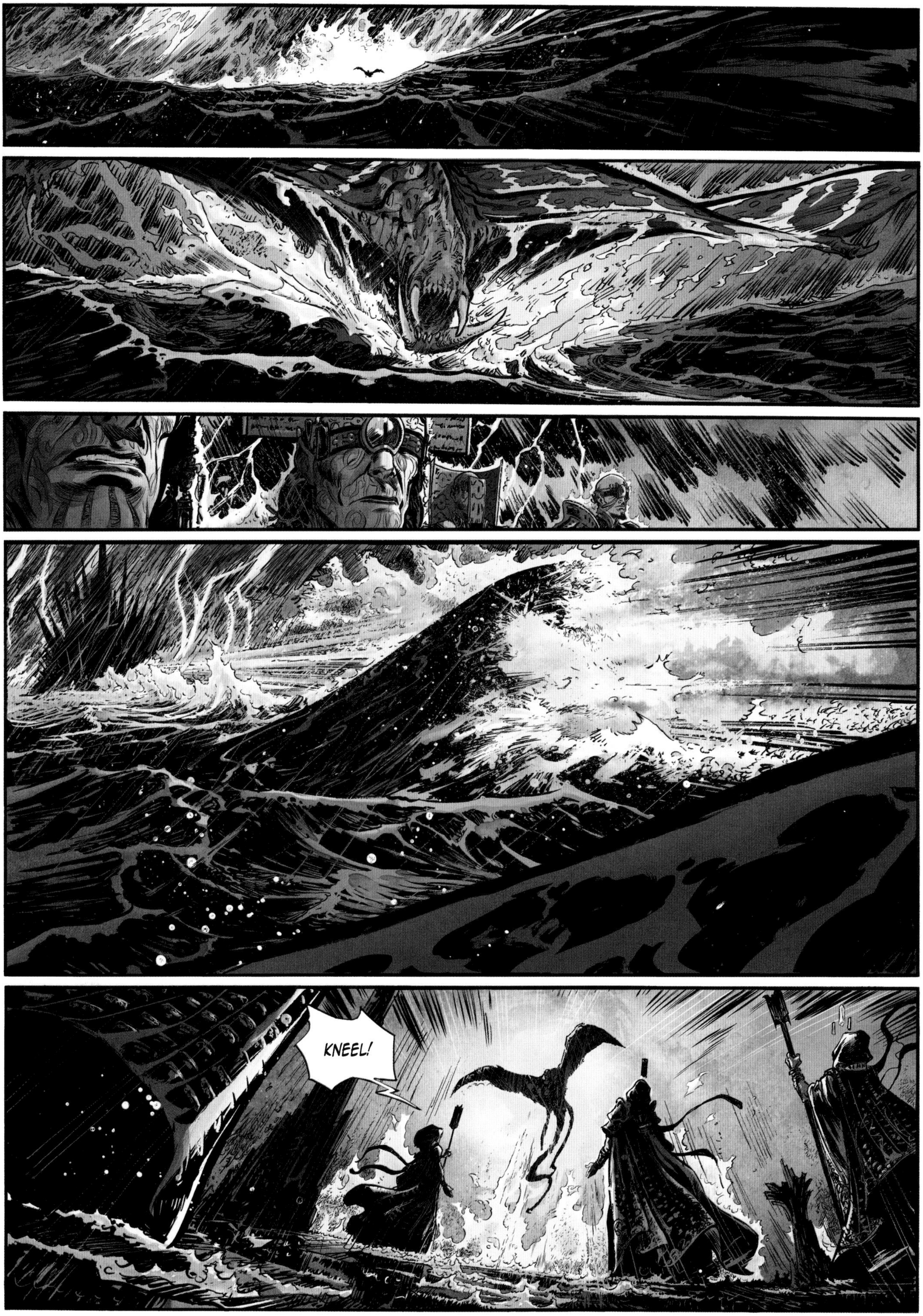
KNEEL!

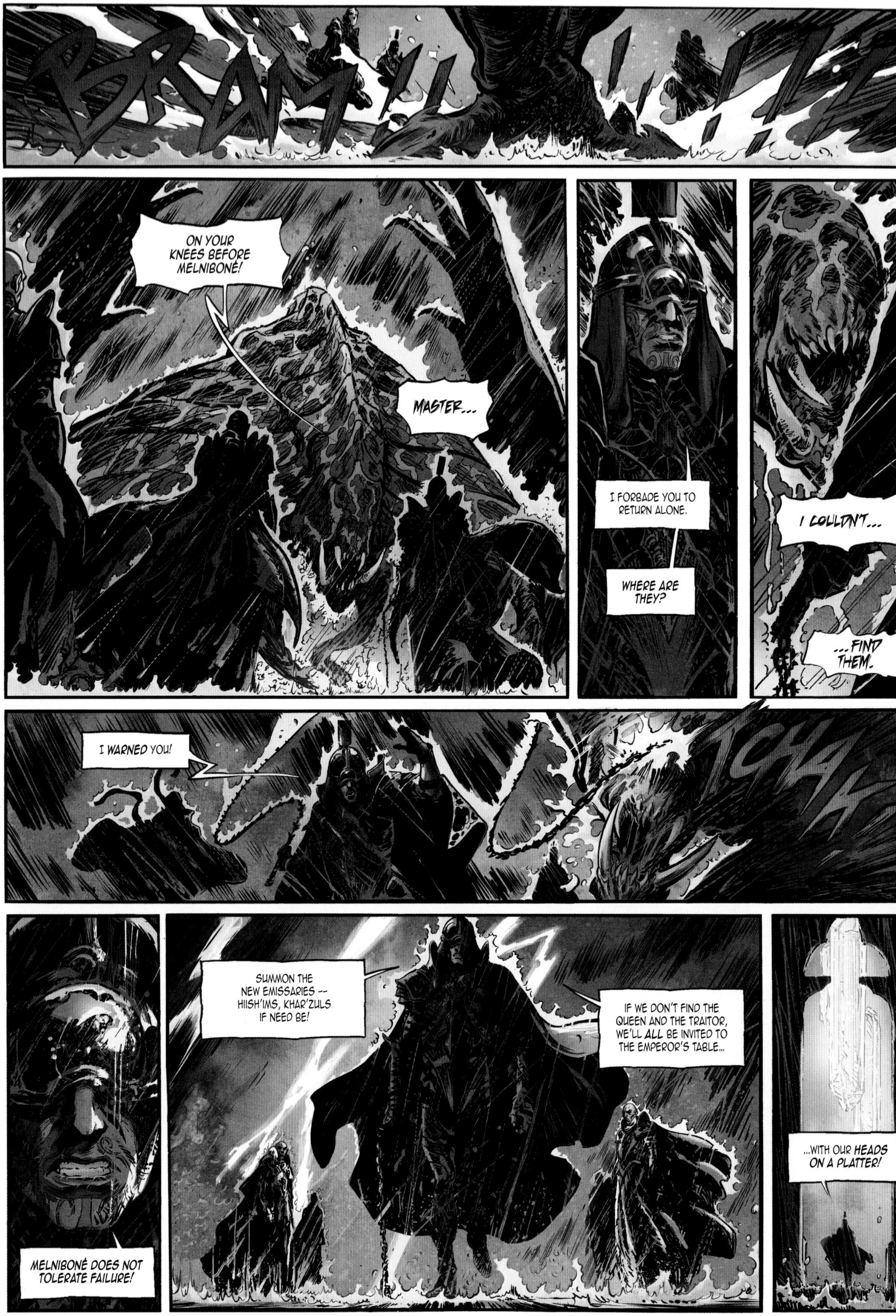
BRAM!!
ON YOUR KNEES BEFORE MELNIBONÉ!
MASTER...
I FORBADE YOU TO RETURN ALONE.
WHERE ARE THEY?
I COULDN'T...
...FIND THEM.
I WARNED YOU!
MELNIBONÉ DOES NOT TOLERATE FAILURE!
SUMMON THE NEW EMISSARIES -- HIISH'IMS, KHAR'ZULS IF NEED BE!
IF WE DON'T FIND THE QUEEN AND THE TRAITOR, WE'LL ALL BE INVITED TO THE EMPEROR'S TABLE...
...WITH OUR HEADS ON A PLATTER!

NOTHING.

NOTHING!

DOCTOR JEST...

TELL ME YOU'VE GOT BETTER NEWS FOR ME THAN THIS STINKING HEAP OF *USELESS GUTS*...

THE LAST VOOR'EKH JUST RETURNED TO THE PALACE. OUR DEMONS HAVE FOUND NO TRACE OF THEM IN THE HUMAN LANDS TO THE SOUTH AND EAST, BUT TOMORROW WE SHALL SEND OUT NEW--

TOMORROW?

TOMORROW?!

MUST OUR EMPEROR CONTAIN HIS RAGE FOR YET *ANOTHER* DAY?

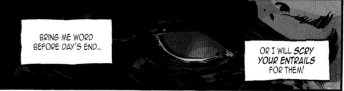

BRING ME WORD BEFORE DAY'S END...

OR I WILL *SCRY YOUR ENTRAILS* FOR THEM!

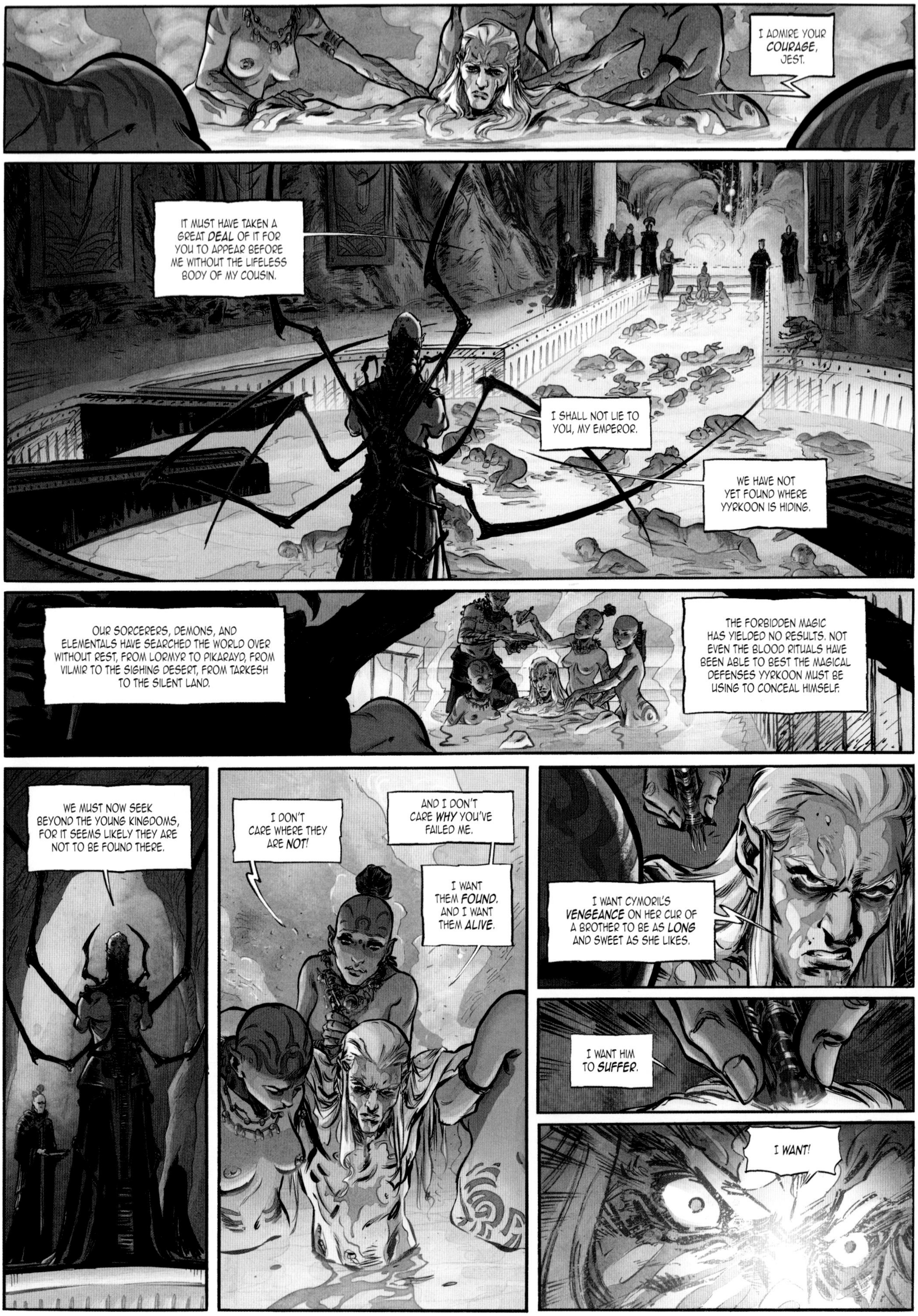
I ADMIRE YOUR COURAGE, JEST.
IT MUST HAVE TAKEN A GREAT DEAL OF IT FOR YOU TO APPEAR BEFORE ME WITHOUT THE LIFELESS BODY OF MY COUSIN.
I SHALL NOT LIE TO YOU, MY EMPEROR.
WE HAVE NOT YET FOUND WHERE YYRKOON IS HIDING.
OUR SORCERERS, DEMONS, AND ELEMENTALS HAVE SEARCHED THE WORLD OVER WITHOUT REST, FROM LORMYR TO PIKARAYD, FROM VILMIR TO THE SIGHING DESERT, FROM TARKESH TO THE SILENT LAND.
THE FORBIDDEN MAGIC HAS YIELDED NO RESULTS. NOT EVEN THE BLOOD RITUALS HAVE BEEN ABLE TO BEST THE MAGICAL DEFENSES YYRKOON MUST BE USING TO CONCEAL HIMSELF.
WE MUST NOW SEEK BEYOND THE YOUNG KINGDOMS, FOR IT SEEMS LIKELY THEY ARE NOT TO BE FOUND THERE.
I DON'T CARE WHERE THEY ARE NOT!
AND I DON'T CARE WHY YOU'VE FAILED ME.
I WANT THEM FOUND, AND I WANT THEM ALIVE.
I WANT CYMORIL'S VENGEANCE ON HER CUR OF A BROTHER TO BE AS LONG AND SWEET AS SHE LIKES.
I WANT HIM TO SUFFER.
I WANT!

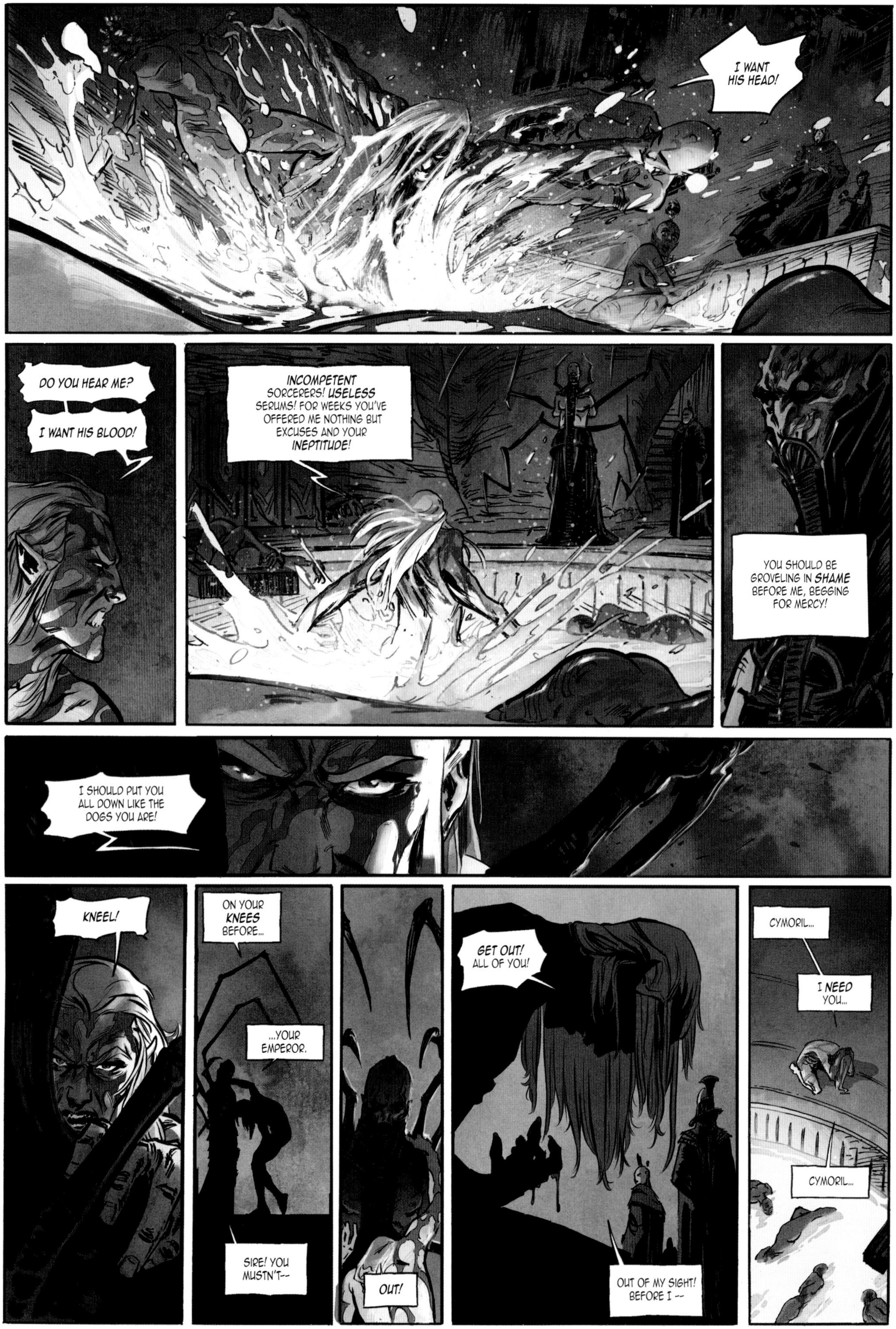
I WANT HIS HEAD!
DO YOU HEAR ME?
I WANT HIS BLOOD!
INCOMPETENT SORCERERS! USELESS SERUMS! FOR WEEKS YOU'VE OFFERED ME NOTHING BUT EXCUSES AND YOUR INEPTITUDE!
YOU SHOULD BE GROVELING IN SHAME BEFORE ME, BEGGING FOR MERCY!
I SHOULD PUT YOU ALL DOWN LIKE THE DOGS YOU ARE!
KNEEL!
ON YOUR KNEES BEFORE...
...YOUR EMPEROR.
SIRE! YOU MUSTN'T--
OUT!
GET OUT! ALL OF YOU!
OUT OF MY SIGHT! BEFORE I --
CYMORIL...
I NEED YOU...
CYMORIL...

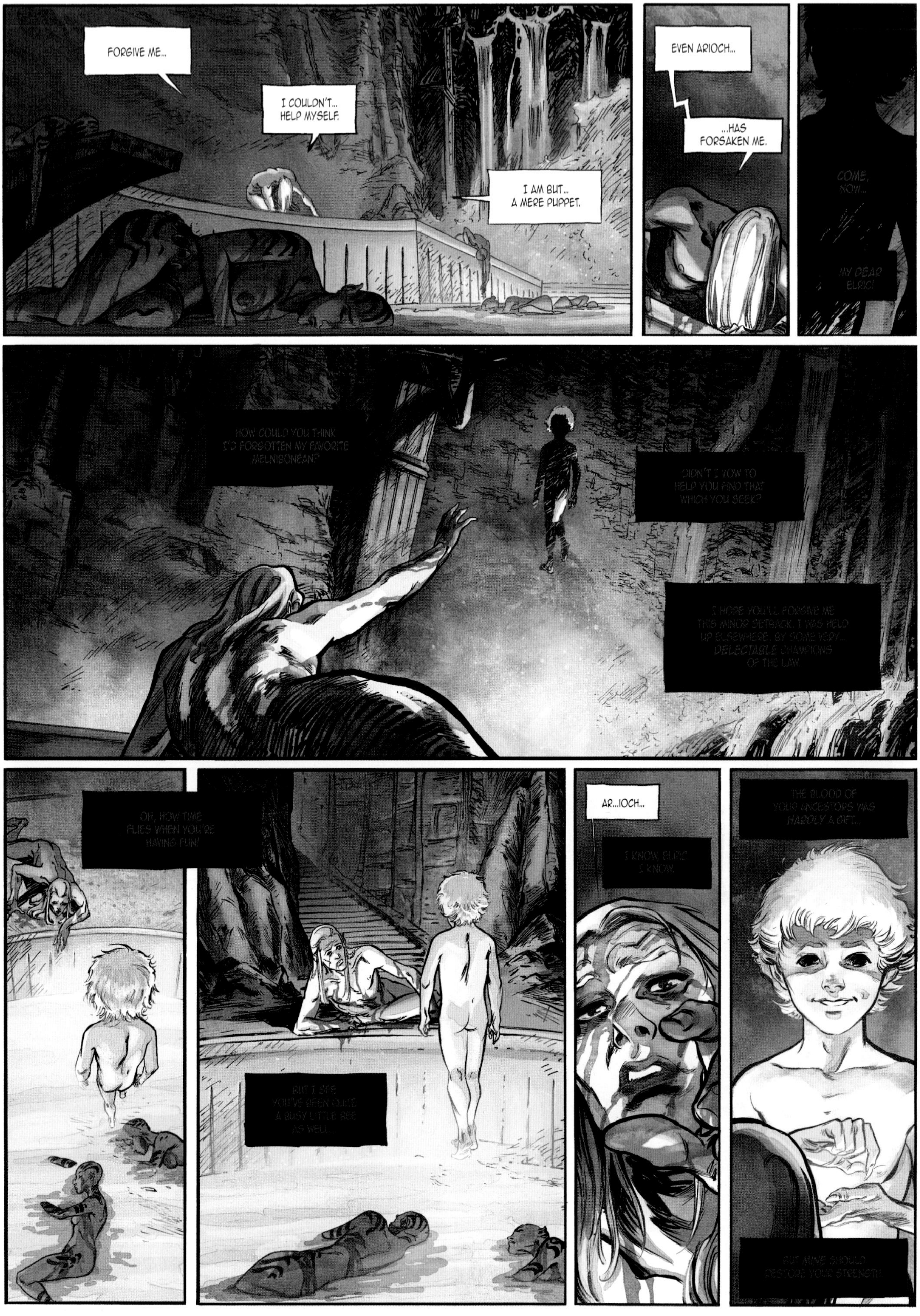
FORGIVE ME...
I COULDN'T... HELP MYSELF.
I AM BUT... A MERE PUPPET.
EVEN ARIOCH...
...HAS FORSAKEN ME.
COME, NOW...
MY DEAR ELRIC!
HOW COULD YOU THINK I'D FORGOTTEN MY FAVORITE MELNIBONÉAN?
DIDN'T I VOW TO HELP YOU FIND THAT WHICH YOU SEEK?
I HOPE YOU'LL FORGIVE ME THIS MINOR SETBACK. I WAS HELD UP ELSEWHERE, BY SOME VERY... DELECTABLE CHAMPIONS OF THE LAW.
OH, HOW TIME FLIES WHEN YOU'RE HAVING FUN!
BUT I SEE YOU'VE BEEN QUITE A BUSY LITTLE BEE AS WELL...
AR...IOCH...
I KNOW, ELRIC. I KNOW.
THE BLOOD OF YOUR ANCESTORS WAS HARDLY A GIFT...
BUT MINE SHOULD RESTORE YOUR STRENGTH.

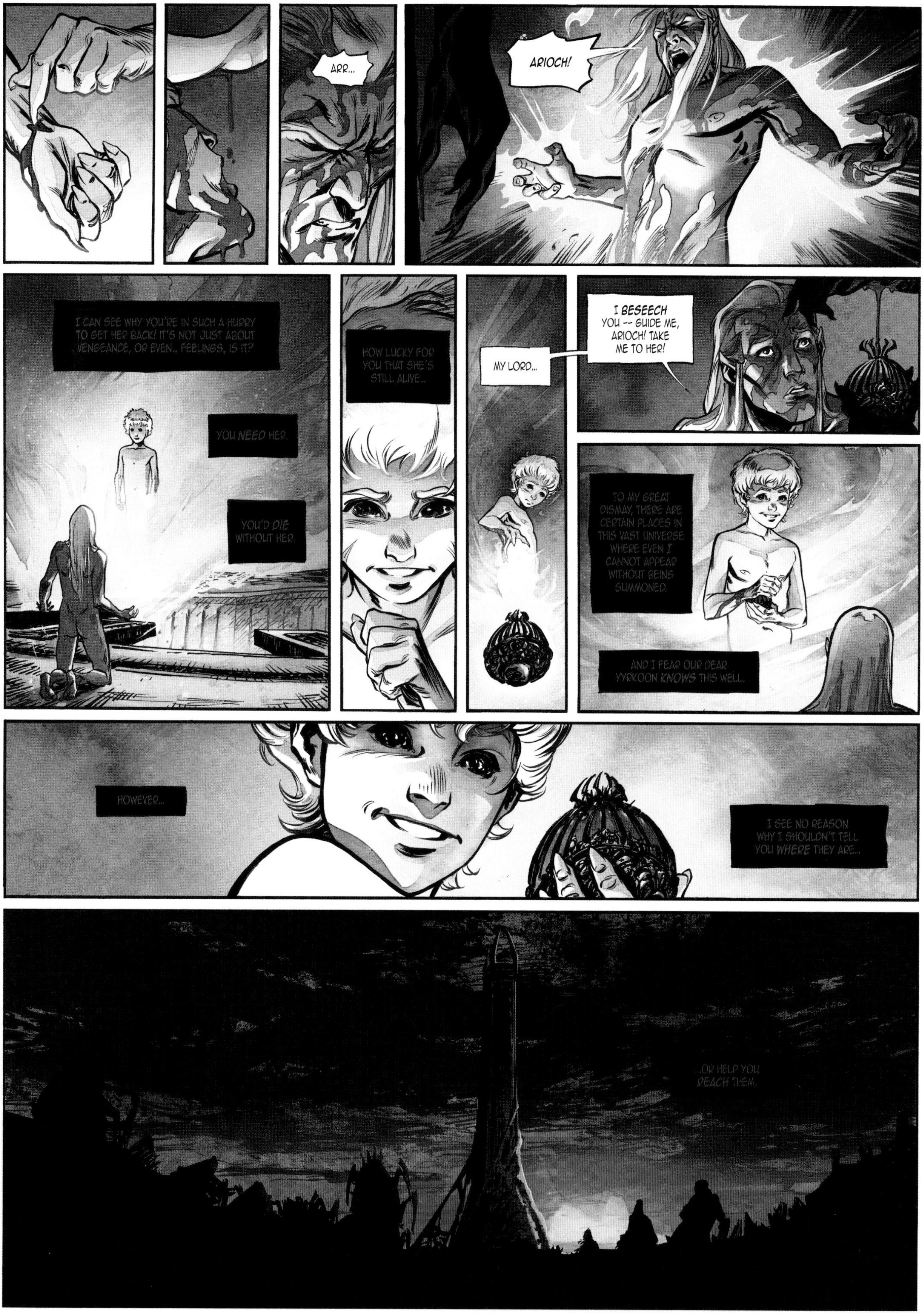
ARR...
ARIOCH!
I CAN SEE WHY YOU'RE IN SUCH A HURRY TO GET HER BACK! IT'S NOT JUST ABOUT VENGEANCE, OR EVEN... FEELINGS, IS IT?
YOU NEED HER.
YOU'D DIE WITHOUT HER.
HOW LUCKY FOR YOU THAT SHE'S STILL ALIVE...
MY LORD...
I BESEECH YOU -- GUIDE ME, ARIOCH! TAKE ME TO HER!
TO MY GREAT DISMAY, THERE ARE CERTAIN PLACES IN THIS VAST UNIVERSE WHERE EVEN I CANNOT APPEAR WITHOUT BEING SUMMONED.
AND I FEAR OUR DEAR YYRKOON KNOWS THIS WELL.
HOWEVER...
I SEE NO REASON WHY I SHOULDN'T TELL YOU WHERE THEY ARE...
...OR HELP YOU REACH THEM.

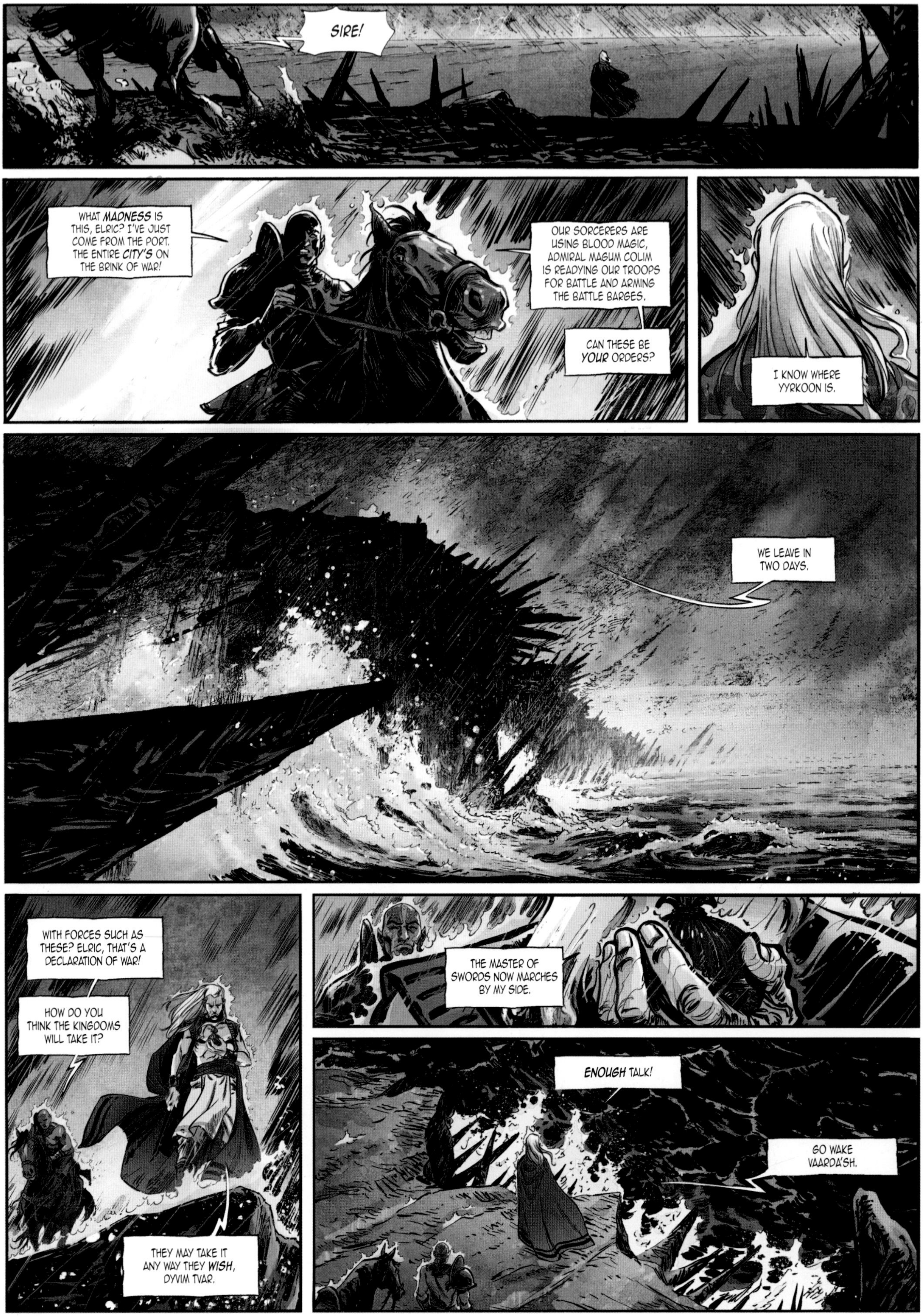
SIRE!
WHAT MADNESS IS THIS, ELRIC? I'VE JUST COME FROM THE PORT. THE ENTIRE CITY'S ON THE BRINK OF WAR!
OUR SORCERERS ARE USING BLOOD MAGIC, ADMIRAL MAGUM COLIM IS READYING OUR TROOPS FOR BATTLE AND ARMING THE BATTLE BARGES.
CAN THESE BE YOUR ORDERS?
I KNOW WHERE YYRKOON IS.
WE LEAVE IN TWO DAYS.
WITH FORCES SUCH AS THESE? ELRIC, THAT'S A DECLARATION OF WAR!
HOW DO YOU THINK THE KINGDOMS WILL TAKE IT?
THEY MAY TAKE IT ANY WAY THEY WISH, DYVIM TVAR.
THE MASTER OF SWORDS NOW MARCHES BY MY SIDE.
ENOUGH TALK!
GO WAKE VAARDA'SH.

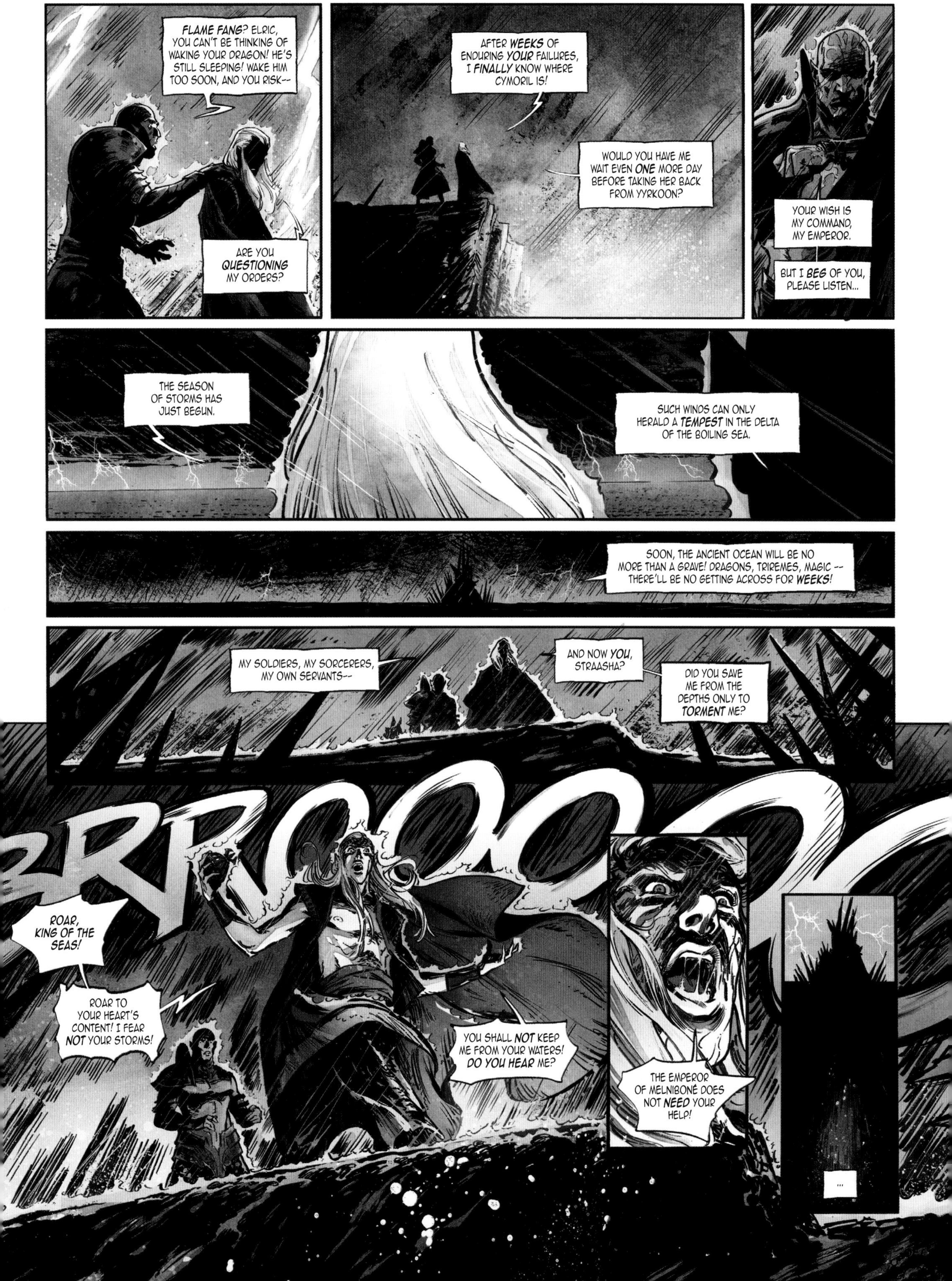

FLAME FANG? ELRIC, YOU CAN'T BE THINKING OF WAKING YOUR DRAGON! HE'S STILL SLEEPING! WAKE HIM TOO SOON, AND YOU RISK--
ARE YOU QUESTIONING MY ORDERS?
AFTER WEEKS OF ENDURING YOUR FAILURES, I FINALLY KNOW WHERE CYMORIL IS!
WOULD YOU HAVE ME WAIT EVEN ONE MORE DAY BEFORE TAKING HER BACK FROM YYRKOON?
YOUR WISH IS MY COMMAND, MY EMPEROR.
BUT I BEG OF YOU, PLEASE LISTEN...
THE SEASON OF STORMS HAS JUST BEGUN.
SUCH WINDS CAN ONLY HERALD A TEMPEST IN THE DELTA OF THE BOILING SEA.
SOON, THE ANCIENT OCEAN WILL BE NO MORE THAN A GRAVE! DRAGONS, TRIREMES, MAGIC -- THERE'LL BE NO GETTING ACROSS FOR WEEKS!
MY SOLDIERS, MY SORCERERS, MY OWN SERVANTS--
AND NOW YOU, STRAASHA?
DID YOU SAVE ME FROM THE DEPTHS ONLY TO TORMENT ME?
BRROOOO
ROAR, KING OF THE SEAS!
ROAR TO YOUR HEART'S CONTENT! I FEAR NOT YOUR STORMS!
YOU SHALL NOT KEEP ME FROM YOUR WATERS! DO YOU HEAR ME?
THE EMPEROR OF MELNIBONÉ DOES NOT NEED YOUR HELP!
...

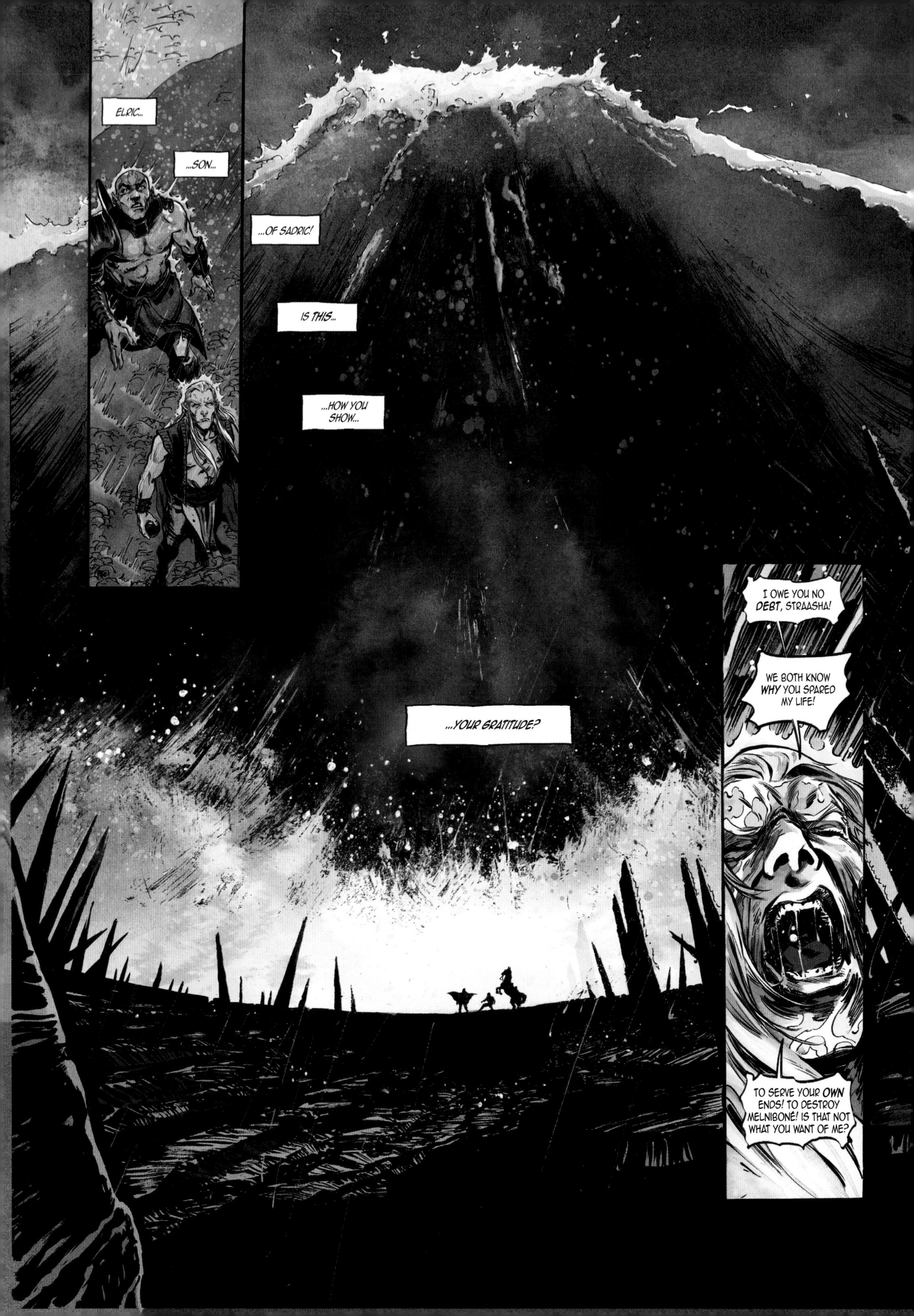
ELRIC...
...SON...
...OF SADRIC!
IS THIS...
...HOW YOU SHOW...
...YOUR GRATITUDE?
I OWE YOU NO DEBT, STRAASHA!
WE BOTH KNOW WHY YOU SPARED MY LIFE!
TO SERVE YOUR OWN ENDS! TO DESTROY MELNIBONÉ! IS THAT NOT WHAT YOU WANT OF ME?

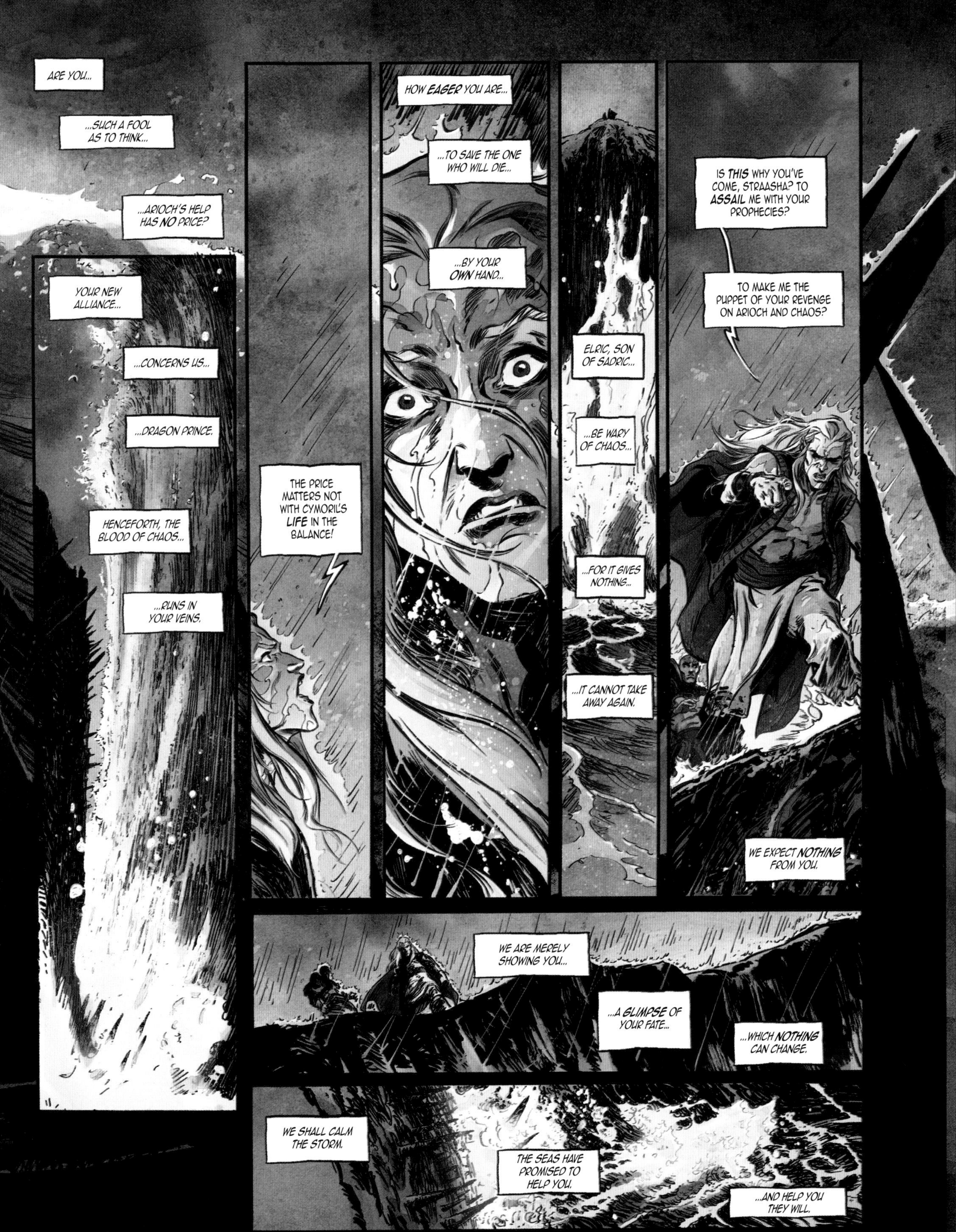
ARE YOU...
...SUCH A FOOL AS TO THINK...
...ARIOCH'S HELP HAS NO PRICE?
YOUR NEW ALLIANCE...
...CONCERNS US...
...DRAGON PRINCE.
HENCEFORTH, THE BLOOD OF CHAOS...
...RUNS IN YOUR VEINS.
THE PRICE MATTERS NOT WITH CYMORIL'S LIFE IN THE BALANCE!
HOW EAGER YOU ARE...
...TO SAVE THE ONE WHO WILL DIE...
...BY YOUR OWN HAND...
ELRIC, SON OF SADRIC...
...BE WARY OF CHAOS...
...FOR IT GIVES NOTHING...
...IT CANNOT TAKE AWAY AGAIN.
IS THIS WHY YOU'VE COME, STRAASHA? TO ASSAIL ME WITH YOUR PROPHECIES?
TO MAKE ME THE PUPPET OF YOUR REVENGE ON ARIOCH AND CHAOS?
WE EXPECT NOTHING FROM YOU.
WE ARE MERELY SHOWING YOU...
...A GLIMPSE OF YOUR FATE...
...WHICH NOTHING CAN CHANGE.
WE SHALL CALM THE STORM.
THE SEAS HAVE PROMISED TO HELP YOU.
...AND HELP YOU THEY WILL.

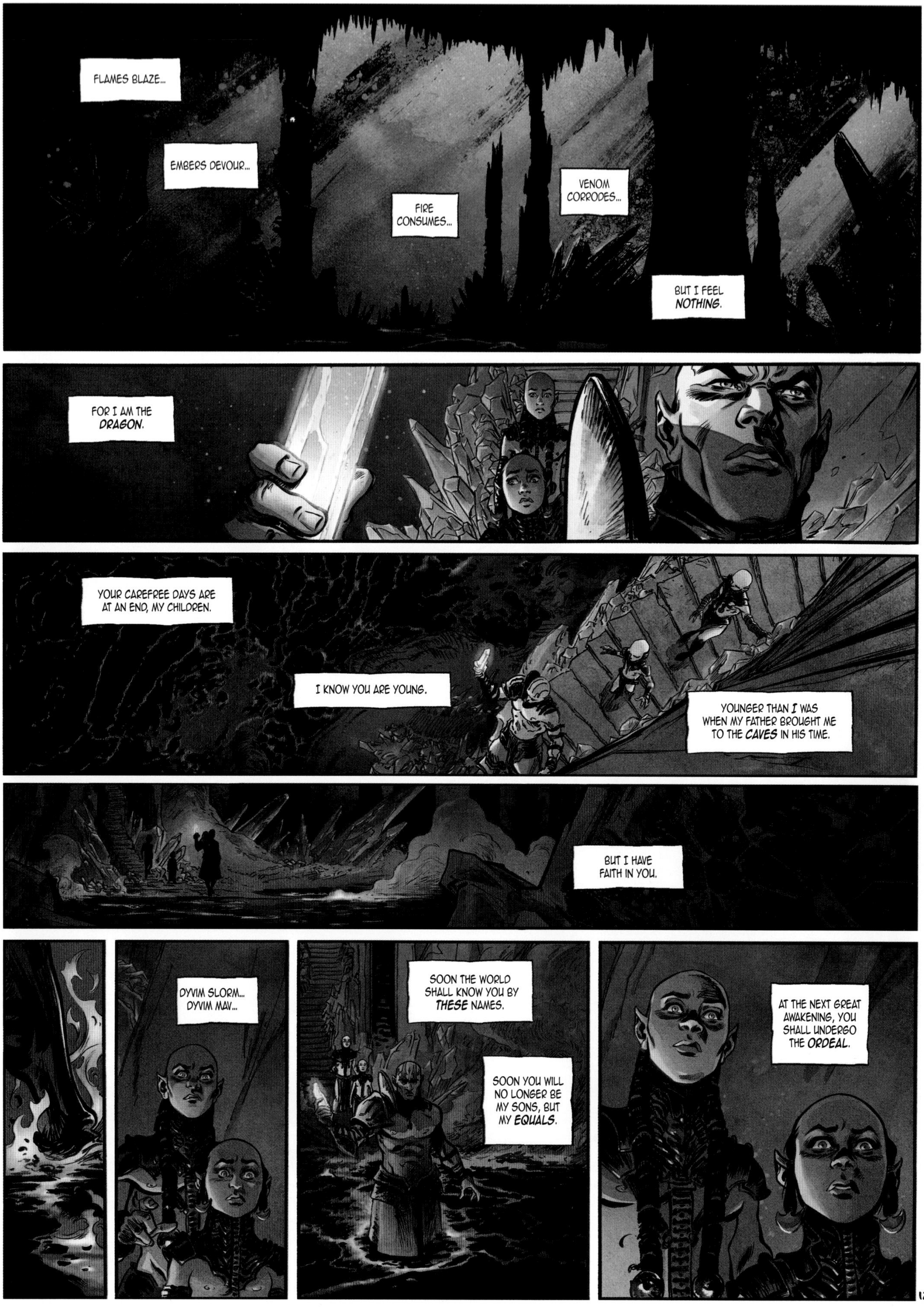

FLAMES BLAZE...
EMBERS DEVOUR...
FIRE CONSUMES...
VENOM CORRODES...
BUT I FEEL NOTHING.
FOR I AM THE DRAGON.
YOUR CAREFREE DAYS ARE AT AN END, MY CHILDREN.
I KNOW YOU ARE YOUNG.
YOUNGER THAN I WAS WHEN MY FATHER BROUGHT ME TO THE CAVES IN HIS TIME.
BUT I HAVE FAITH IN YOU.
DYVIM SLORM... DYVIM MAV...
SOON THE WORLD SHALL KNOW YOU BY THESE NAMES.
SOON YOU WILL NO LONGER BE MY SONS, BUT MY EQUALS.
AT THE NEXT GREAT AWAKENING, YOU SHALL UNDERGO THE ORDEAL.

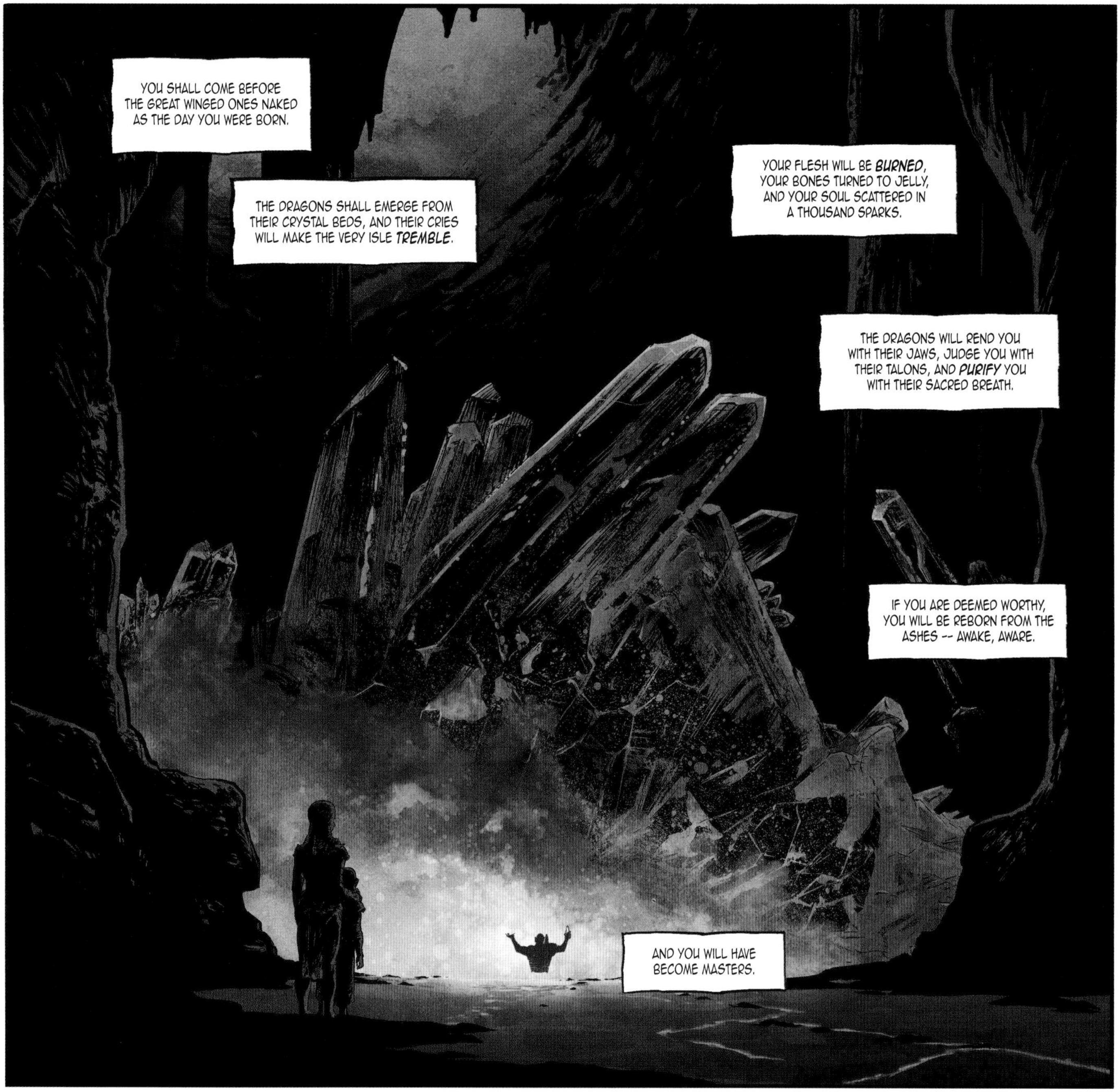
YOU SHALL COME BEFORE THE GREAT WINGED ONES NAKED AS THE DAY YOU WERE BORN.
THE DRAGONS SHALL EMERGE FROM THEIR CRYSTAL BEDS, AND THEIR CRIES WILL MAKE THE VERY ISLE *TREMBLE*.
YOUR FLESH WILL BE *BURNED*, YOUR BONES TURNED TO JELLY, AND YOUR SOUL SCATTERED IN A THOUSAND SPARKS.
THE DRAGONS WILL REND YOU WITH THEIR JAWS, JUDGE YOU WITH THEIR TALONS, AND *PURIFY* YOU WITH THEIR SACRED BREATH.
IF YOU ARE DEEMED WORTHY, YOU WILL BE REBORN FROM THE ASHES -- AWAKE, AWARE.
AND YOU WILL HAVE BECOME MASTERS.
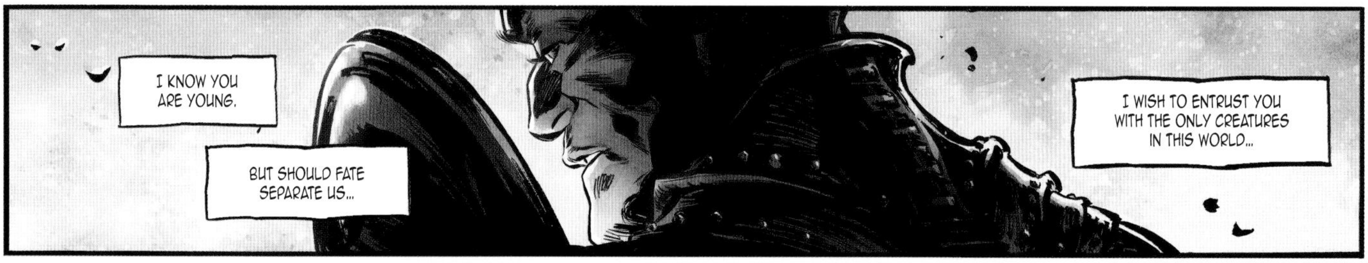
I KNOW YOU ARE YOUNG.
BUT SHOULD FATE SEPARATE US...
I WISH TO ENTRUST YOU WITH THE ONLY CREATURES IN THIS WORLD...
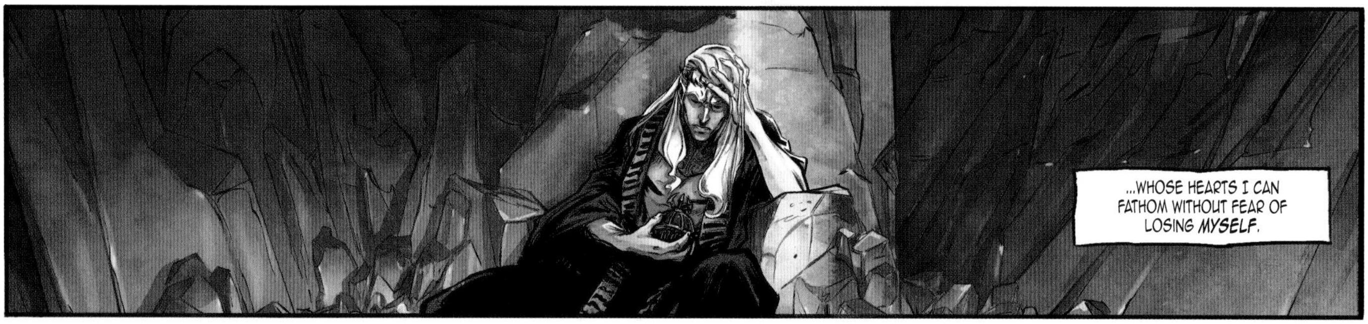
...WHOSE HEARTS I CAN FATHOM WITHOUT FEAR OF LOSING *MYSELF*.

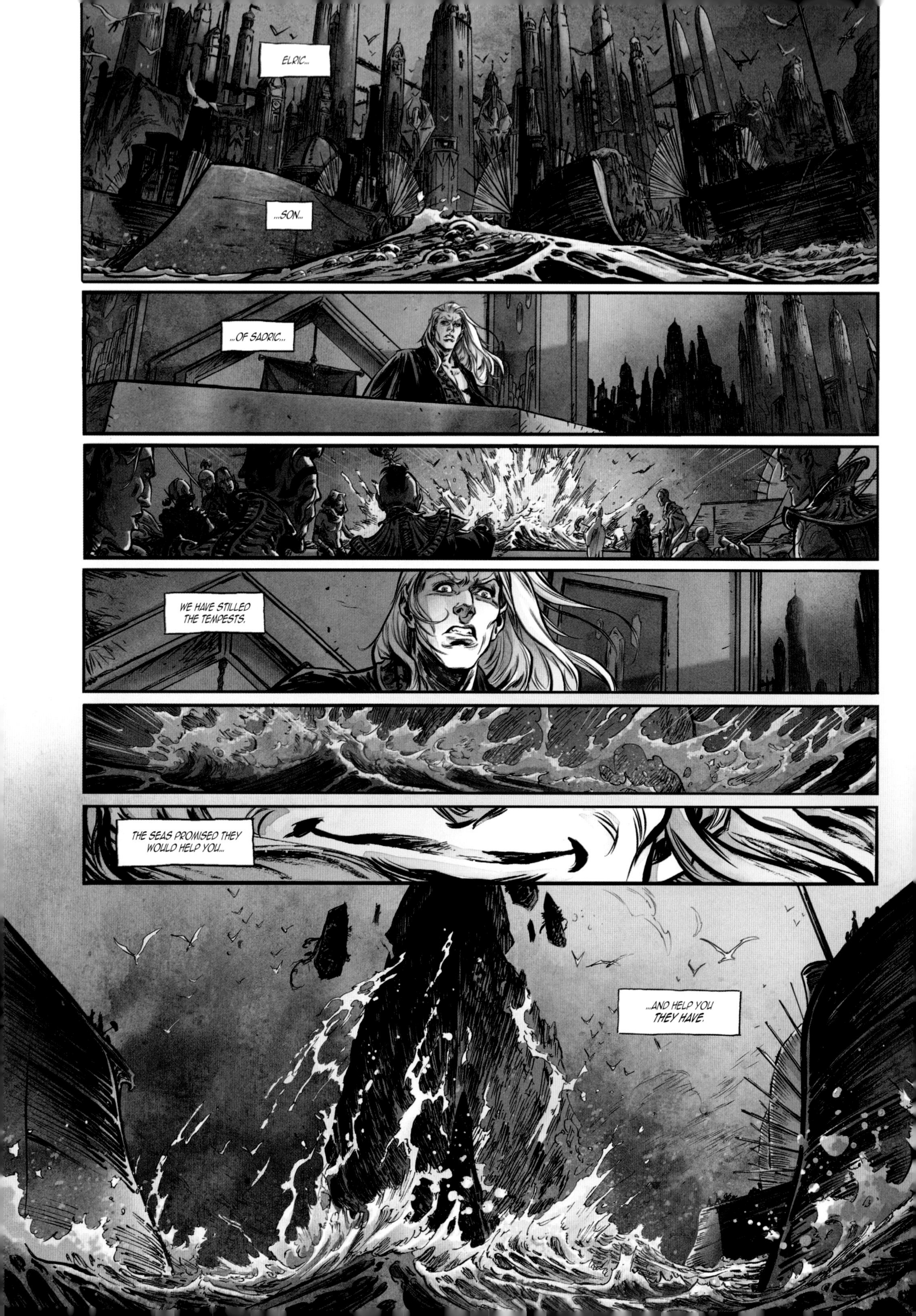
ELRIC...
...SON...
...OF SADRIC...
WE HAVE STILLED THE TEMPESTS.
THE SEAS PROMISED THEY WOULD HELP YOU...
...AND HELP YOU THEY HAVE.

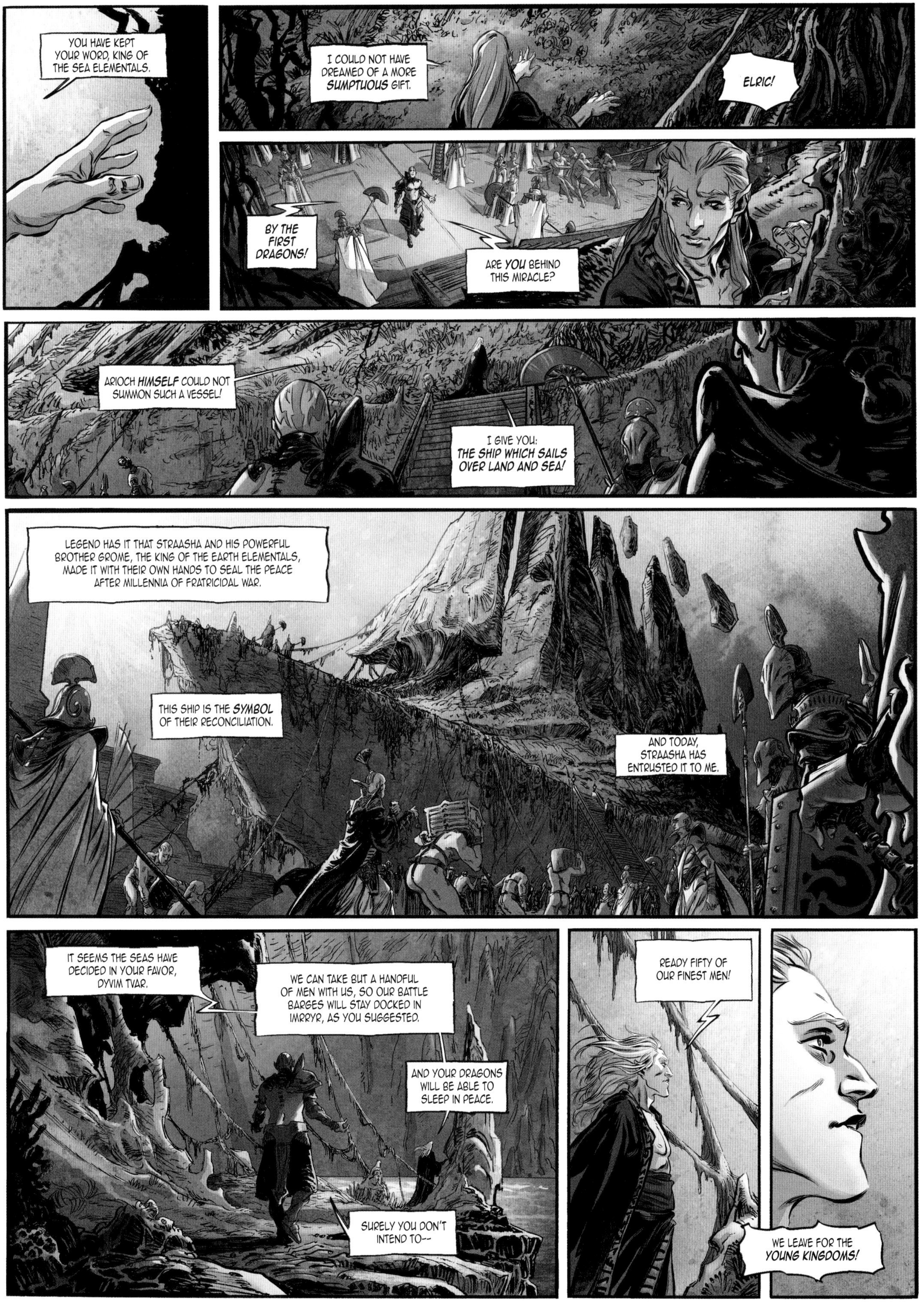
YOU HAVE KEPT YOUR WORD, KING OF THE SEA ELEMENTALS.
I COULD NOT HAVE DREAMED OF A MORE SUMPTUOUS GIFT.
ELRIC!
BY THE FIRST DRAGONS!
ARE YOU BEHIND THIS MIRACLE?
ARIOCH HIMSELF COULD NOT SUMMON SUCH A VESSEL!
I GIVE YOU: THE SHIP WHICH SAILS OVER LAND AND SEA!
LEGEND HAS IT THAT STRAASHA AND HIS POWERFUL BROTHER GROME, THE KING OF THE EARTH ELEMENTALS, MADE IT WITH THEIR OWN HANDS TO SEAL THE PEACE AFTER MILLENNIA OF FRATRICIDAL WAR.
THIS SHIP IS THE SYMBOL OF THEIR RECONCILIATION.
AND TODAY, STRAASHA HAS ENTRUSTED IT TO ME.
IT SEEMS THE SEAS HAVE DECIDED IN YOUR FAVOR, DYVIM TVAR.
WE CAN TAKE BUT A HANDFUL OF MEN WITH US, SO OUR BATTLE BARGES WILL STAY DOCKED IN IMRRYR, AS YOU SUGGESTED.
AND YOUR DRAGONS WILL BE ABLE TO SLEEP IN PEACE.
SURELY YOU DON'T INTEND TO--
READY FIFTY OF OUR FINEST MEN!
WE LEAVE FOR THE YOUNG KINGDOMS!

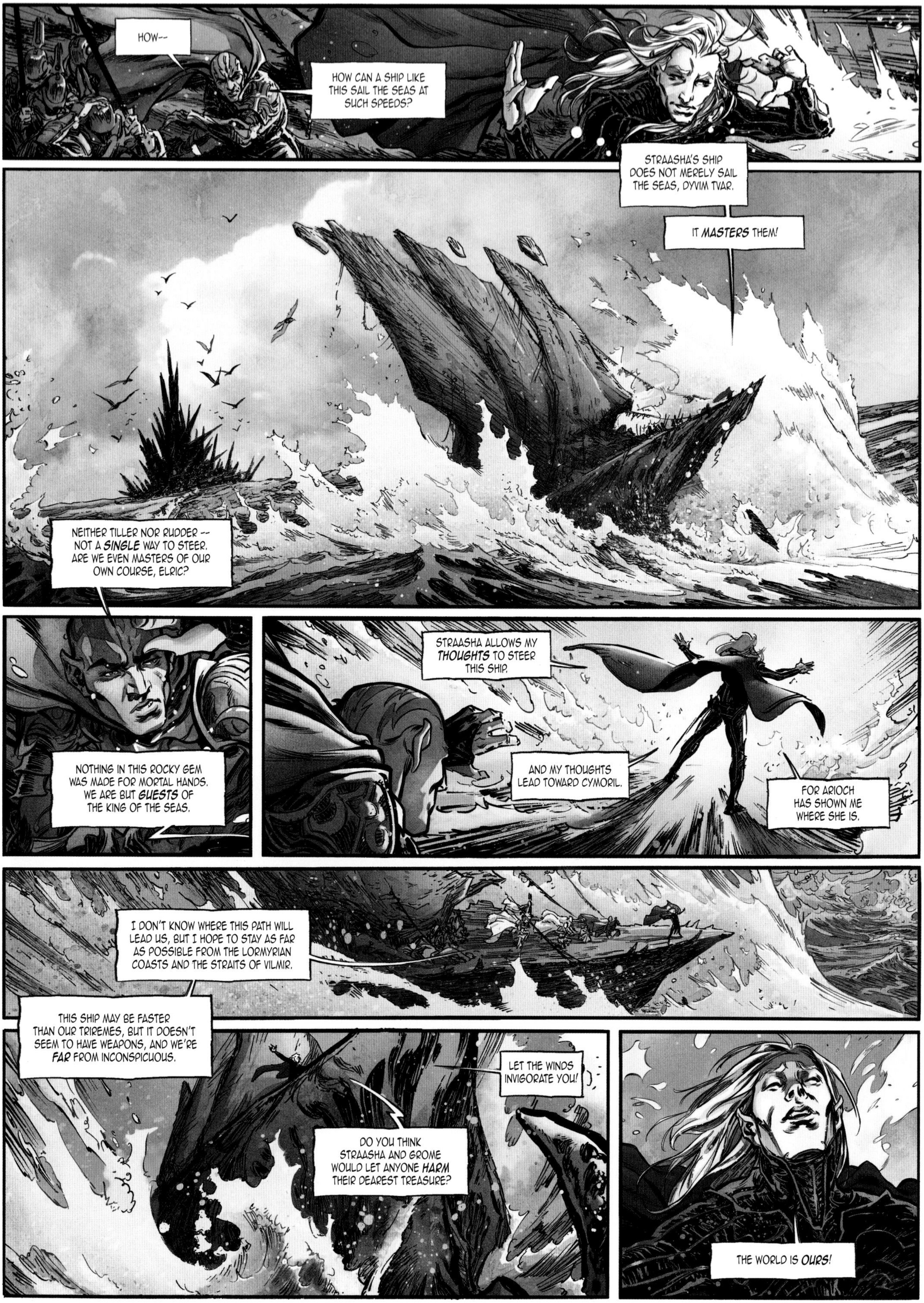

HOW--
HOW CAN A SHIP LIKE THIS SAIL THE SEAS AT SUCH SPEEDS?
STRAASHA'S SHIP DOES NOT MERELY SAIL THE SEAS, DYVIM TVAR.
IT MASTERS THEM!
NEITHER TILLER NOR RUDDER -- NOT A SINGLE WAY TO STEER. ARE WE EVEN MASTERS OF OUR OWN COURSE, ELRIC?
NOTHING IN THIS ROCKY GEM WAS MADE FOR MORTAL HANDS. WE ARE BUT GUESTS OF THE KING OF THE SEAS.
STRAASHA ALLOWS MY THOUGHTS TO STEER THIS SHIP.
AND MY THOUGHTS LEAD TOWARD CYMORIL.
FOR ARIOCH HAS SHOWN ME WHERE SHE IS.
I DON'T KNOW WHERE THIS PATH WILL LEAD US, BUT I HOPE TO STAY AS FAR AS POSSIBLE FROM THE LORMYRIAN COASTS AND THE STRAITS OF VILMIR.
THIS SHIP MAY BE FASTER THAN OUR TRIREMES, BUT IT DOESN'T SEEM TO HAVE WEAPONS, AND WE'RE FAR FROM INCONSPICUOUS.
LET THE WINDS INVIGORATE YOU!
DO YOU THINK STRAASHA AND GROME WOULD LET ANYONE HARM THEIR DEAREST TREASURE?
THE WORLD IS OURS!

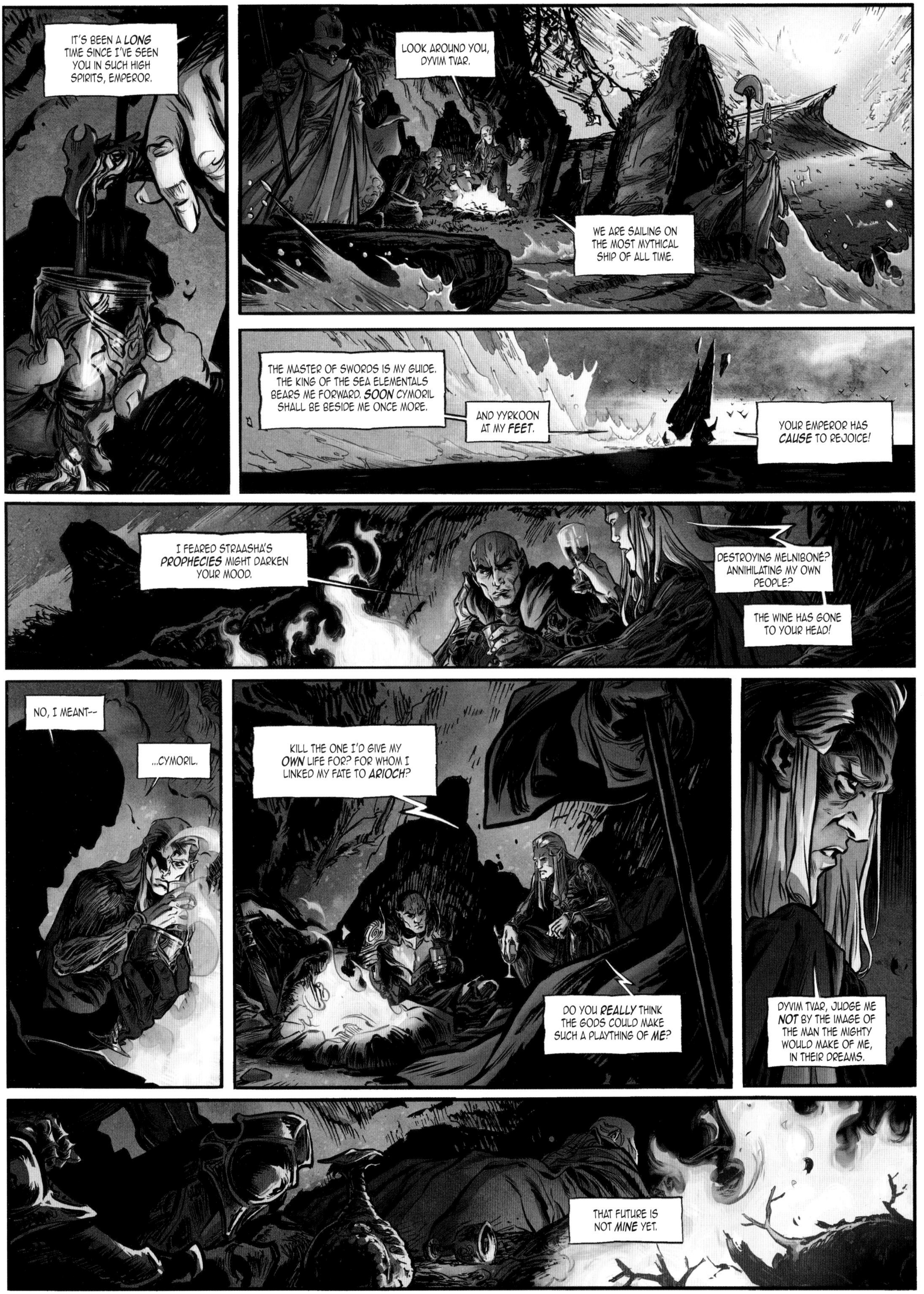
IT'S BEEN A LONG TIME SINCE I'VE SEEN YOU IN SUCH HIGH SPIRITS, EMPEROR.
LOOK AROUND YOU, DYVIM TVAR.
WE ARE SAILING ON THE MOST MYTHICAL SHIP OF ALL TIME.
THE MASTER OF SWORDS IS MY GUIDE. THE KING OF THE SEA ELEMENTALS BEARS ME FORWARD. SOON CYMORIL SHALL BE BESIDE ME ONCE MORE.
AND YYRKOON AT MY FEET.
YOUR EMPEROR HAS CAUSE TO REJOICE!
I FEARED STRAASHA'S PROPHECIES MIGHT DARKEN YOUR MOOD.
DESTROYING MELNIBONÉ? ANNIHILATING MY OWN PEOPLE?
THE WINE HAS GONE TO YOUR HEAD!
NO, I MEANT--
...CYMORIL.
KILL THE ONE I'D GIVE MY OWN LIFE FOR? FOR WHOM I LINKED MY FATE TO ARIOCH?
DO YOU REALLY THINK THE GODS COULD MAKE SUCH A PLAYTHING OF ME?
DYVIM TVAR, JUDGE ME NOT BY THE IMAGE OF THE MAN THE MIGHTY WOULD MAKE OF ME, IN THEIR DREAMS.
THAT FUTURE IS NOT MINE YET.

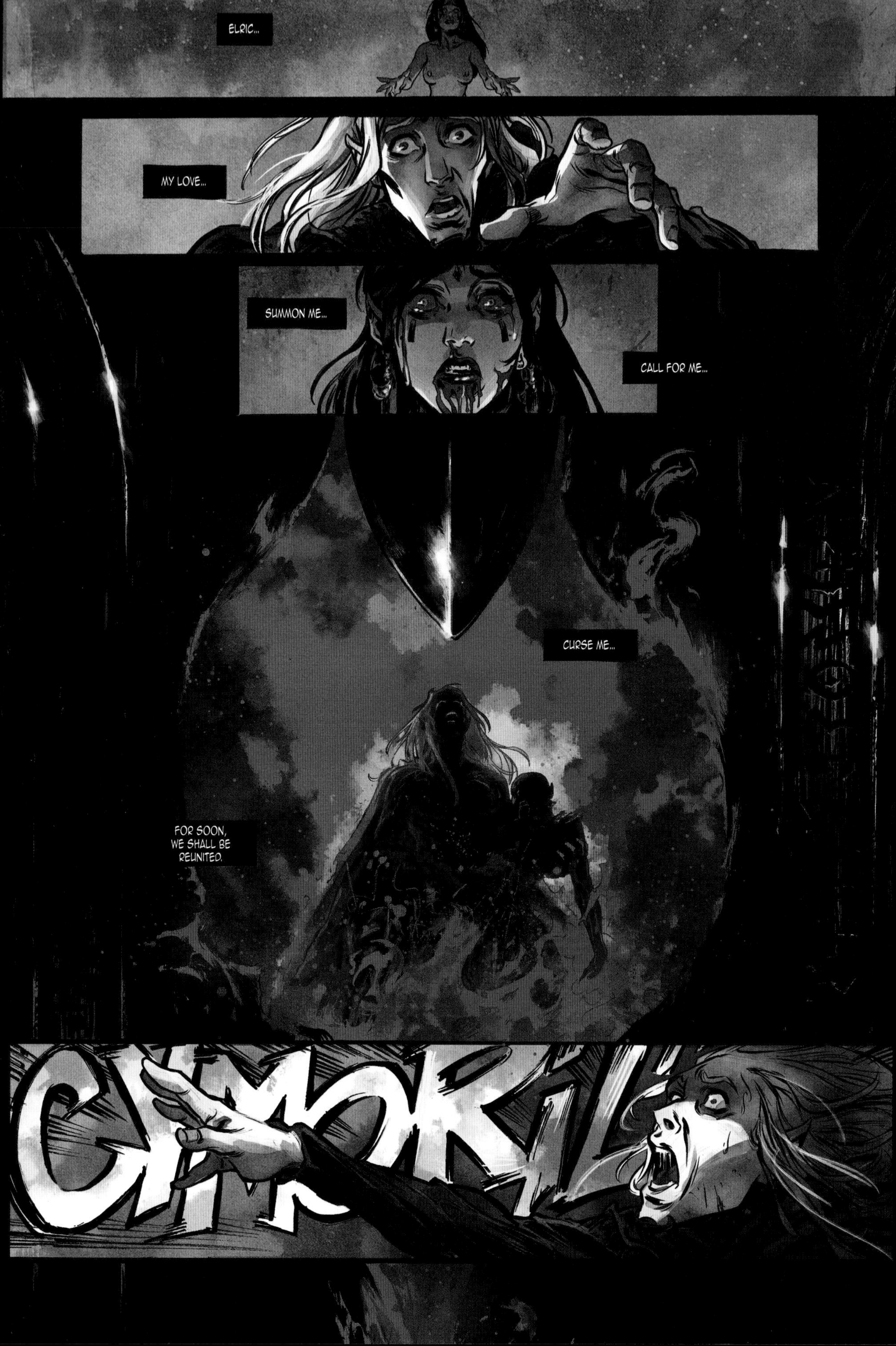
ELRIC...
MY LOVE...
SUMMON ME...
CALL FOR ME...
CURSE ME...
FOR SOON, WE SHALL BE REUNITED.

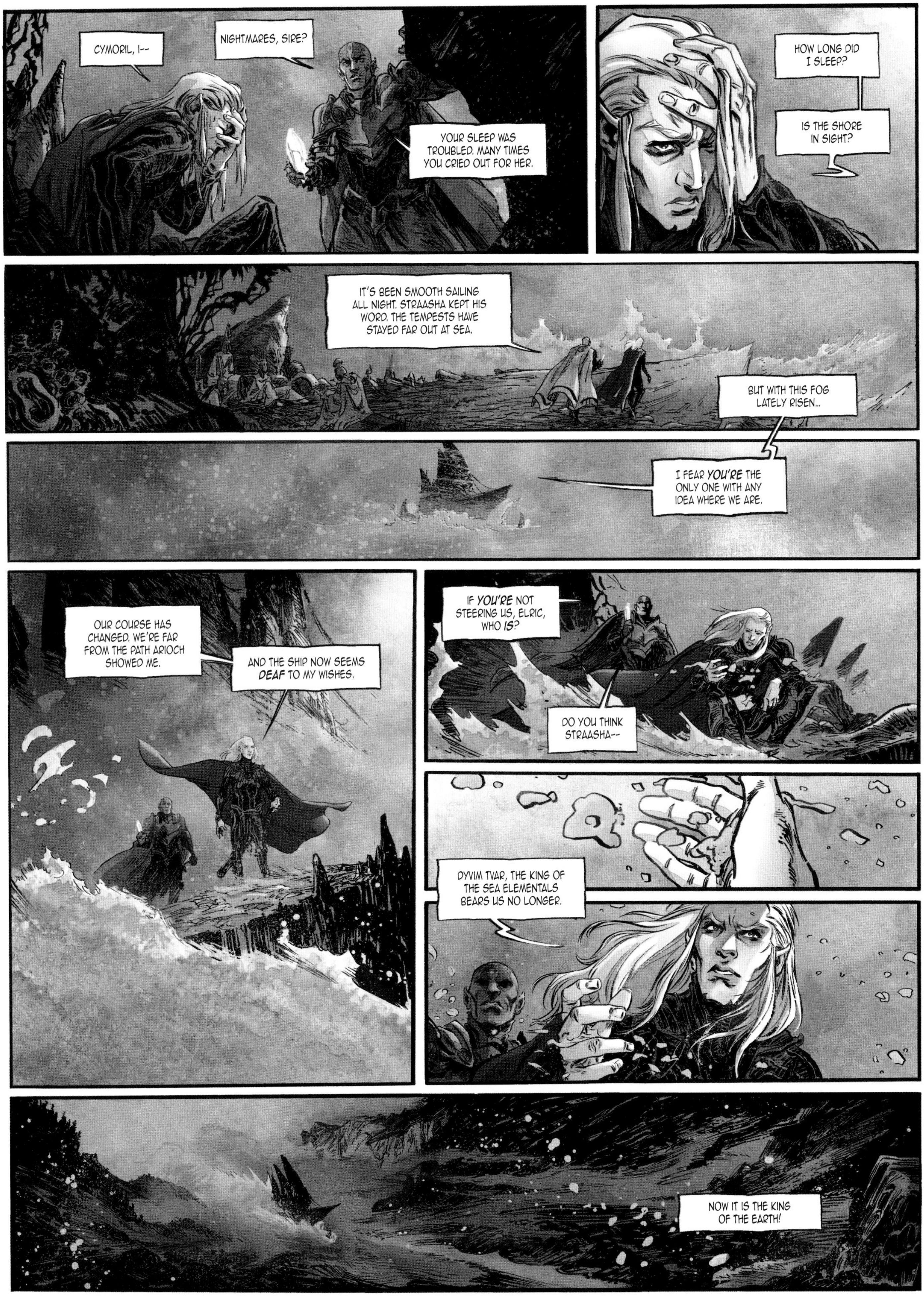
CYMORIL, I--
NIGHTMARES, SIRE?
YOUR SLEEP WAS TROUBLED. MANY TIMES YOU CRIED OUT FOR HER.
HOW LONG DID I SLEEP?
IS THE SHORE IN SIGHT?
IT'S BEEN SMOOTH SAILING ALL NIGHT. STRAASHA KEPT HIS WORD. THE TEMPESTS HAVE STAYED FAR OUT AT SEA.
BUT WITH THIS FOG LATELY RISEN...
I FEAR YOU'RE THE ONLY ONE WITH ANY IDEA WHERE WE ARE.
OUR COURSE HAS CHANGED. WE'RE FAR FROM THE PATH ARIOCH SHOWED ME.
AND THE SHIP NOW SEEMS DEAF TO MY WISHES.
IF YOU'RE NOT STEERING US, ELRIC, WHO IS?
DO YOU THINK STRAASHA--
DYVIM TVAR, THE KING OF THE SEA ELEMENTALS BEARS US NO LONGER.
NOW IT IS THE KING OF THE EARTH!

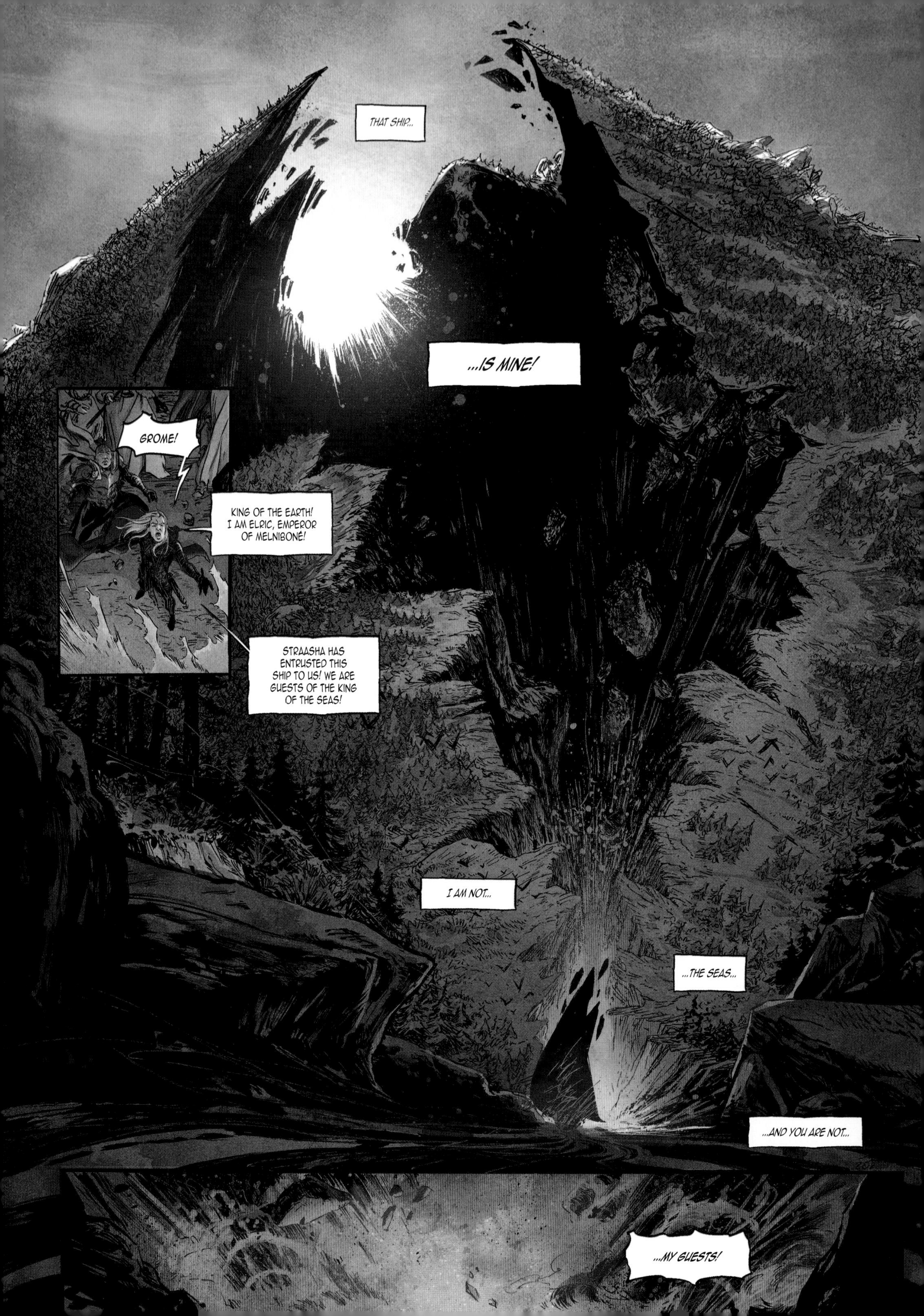
THAT SHIP...
...IS MINE!
GROME!
KING OF THE EARTH! I AM ELRIC, EMPEROR OF MELNIBONÉ!
STRAASHA HAS ENTRUSTED THIS SHIP TO US! WE ARE GUESTS OF THE KING OF THE SEAS!
I AM NOT...
...THE SEAS...
...AND YOU ARE NOT...
...MY GUESTS!

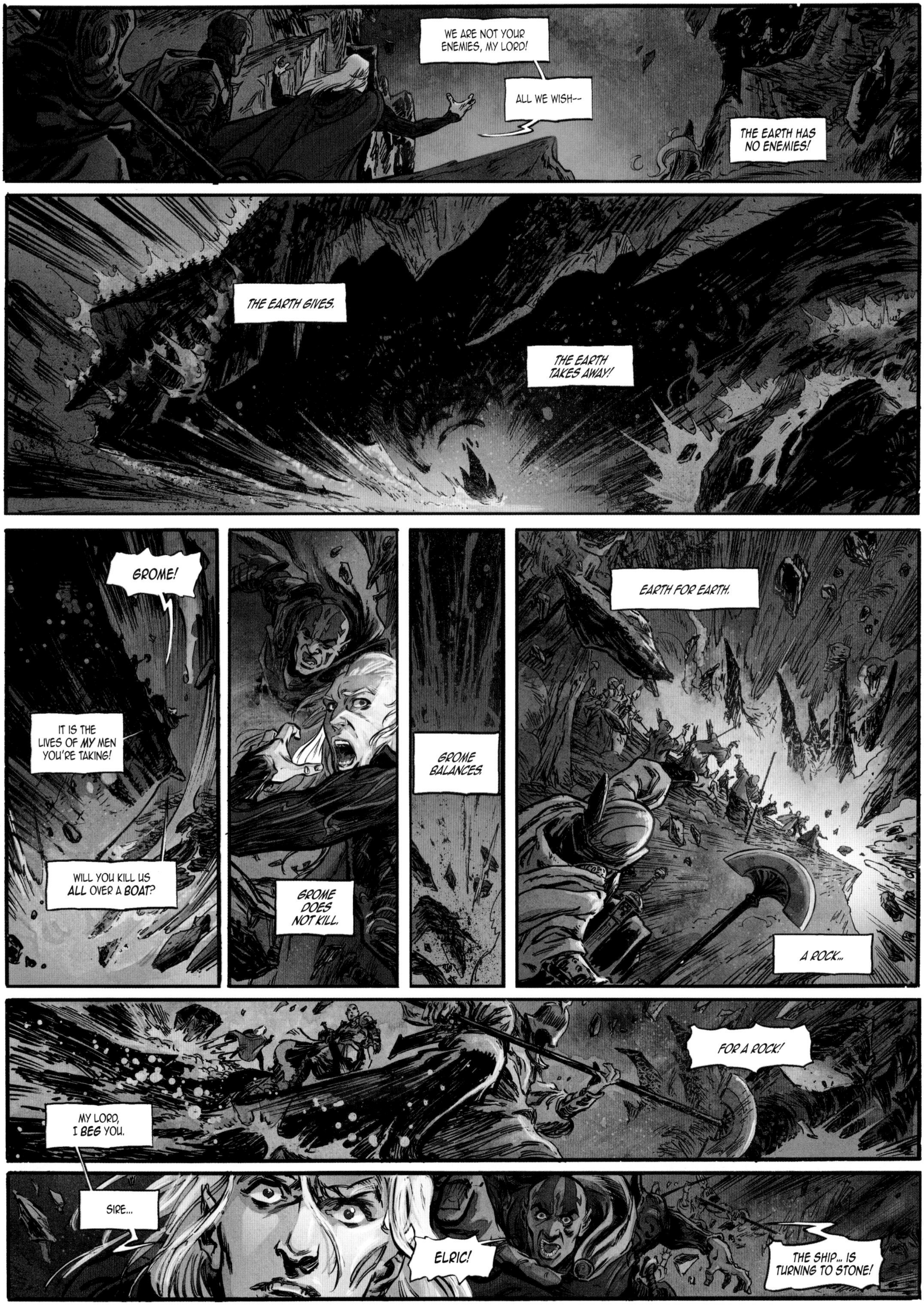
WE ARE NOT YOUR ENEMIES, MY LORD!
ALL WE WISH--
THE EARTH HAS NO ENEMIES!
THE EARTH GIVES.
THE EARTH TAKES AWAY!
GROME!
IT IS THE LIVES OF MY MEN YOU'RE TAKING!
WILL YOU KILL US ALL OVER A BOAT?
GROME DOES NOT KILL.
GROME BALANCES.
EARTH FOR EARTH.
A ROCK...
FOR A ROCK!
MY LORD, I BEG YOU.
SIRE...
ELRIC!
THE SHIP... IS TURNING TO STONE!

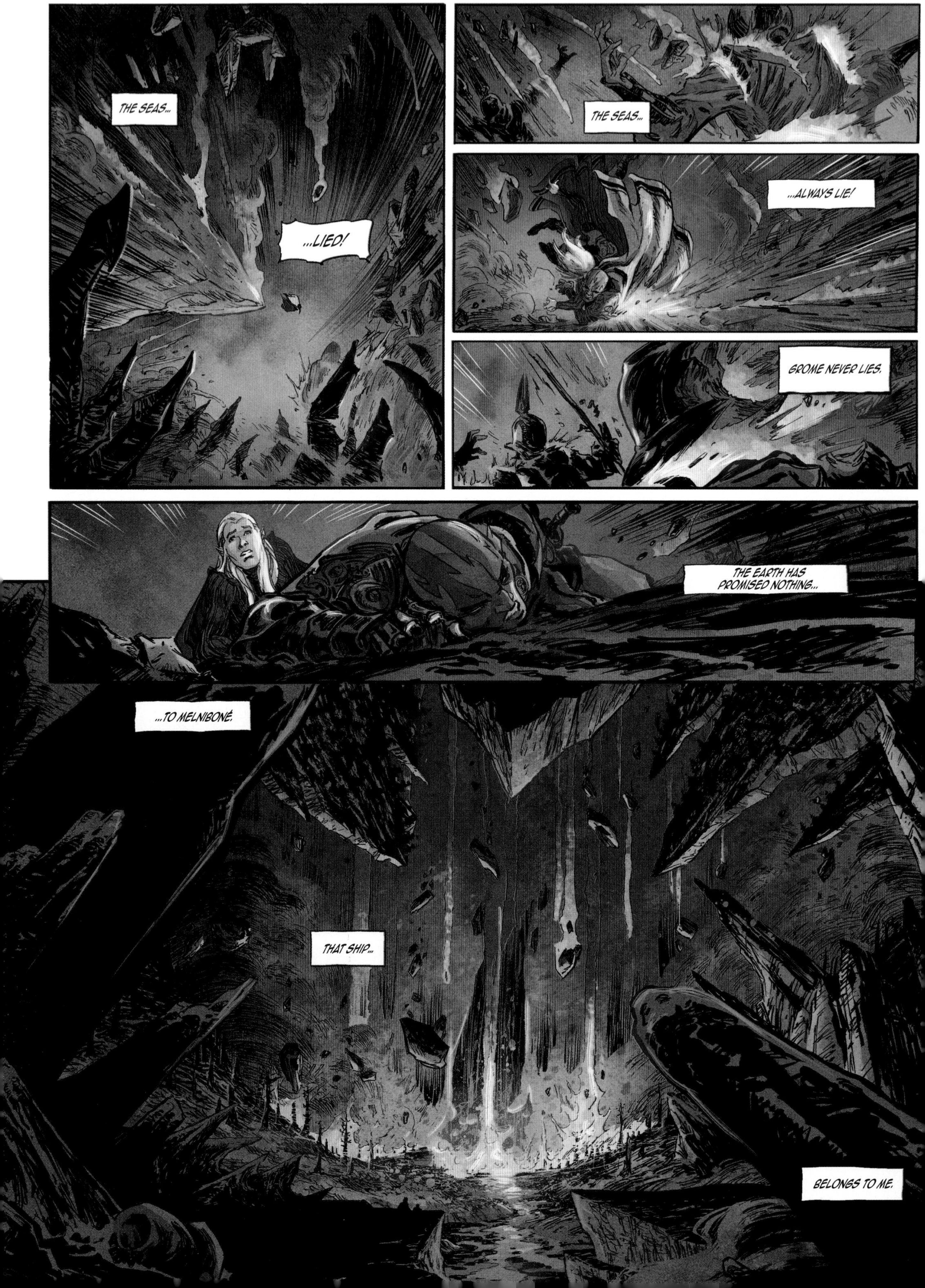
THE SEAS...
...LIED!
THE SEAS...
...ALWAYS LIE!
GROME NEVER LIES.
THE EARTH HAS PROMISED NOTHING...
...TO MELNIBONÉ.
THAT SHIP...
BELONGS TO ME.

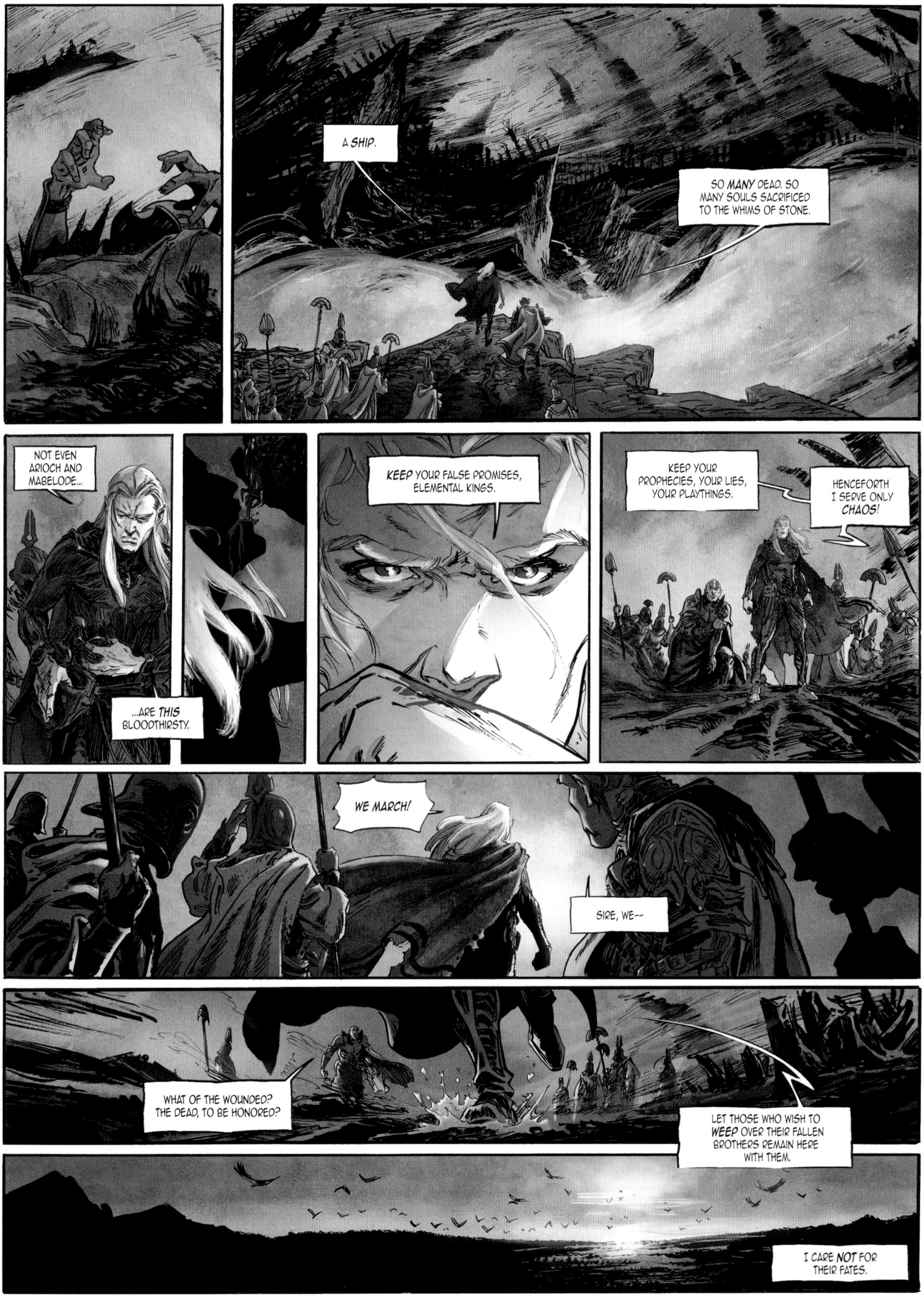
A SHIP.
SO MANY DEAD. SO MANY SOULS SACRIFICED TO THE WHIMS OF STONE.
NOT EVEN ARIOCH AND MABELODE...
...ARE THIS BLOODTHIRSTY.
KEEP YOUR FALSE PROMISES, ELEMENTAL KINGS.
KEEP YOUR PROPHECIES, YOUR LIES, YOUR PLAYTHINGS.
HENCEFORTH I SERVE ONLY CHAOS!
WE MARCH!
SIRE, WE--
WHAT OF THE WOUNDED? THE DEAD, TO BE HONORED?
LET THOSE WHO WISH TO WEEP OVER THEIR FALLEN BROTHERS REMAIN HERE WITH THEM.
I CARE NOT FOR THEIR FATES.

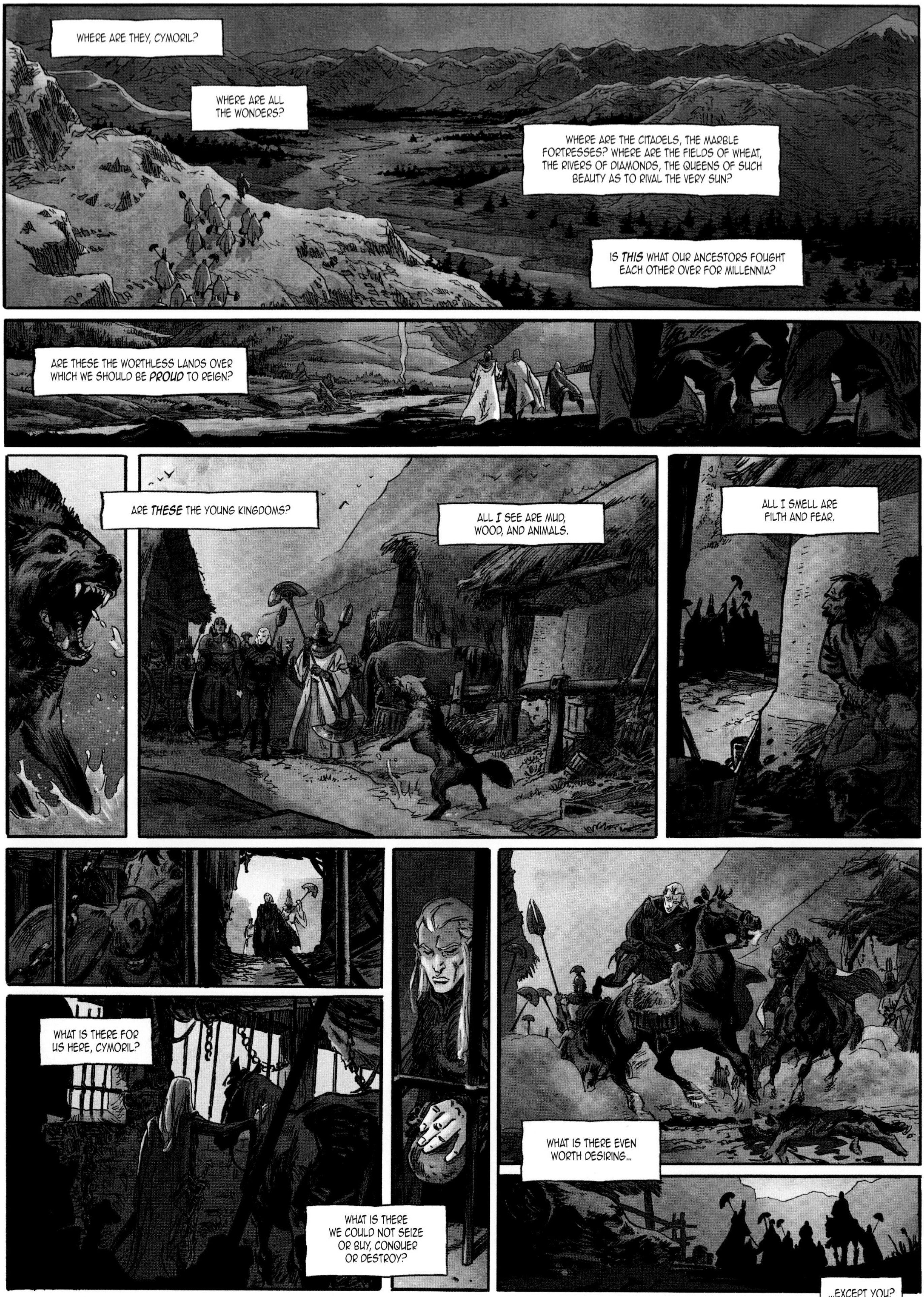
WHERE ARE THEY, CYMORIL?
WHERE ARE ALL THE WONDERS?
WHERE ARE THE CITADELS, THE MARBLE FORTRESSES? WHERE ARE THE FIELDS OF WHEAT, THE RIVERS OF DIAMONDS, THE QUEENS OF SUCH BEAUTY AS TO RIVAL THE VERY SUN?
IS THIS WHAT OUR ANCESTORS FOUGHT EACH OTHER OVER FOR MILLENNIA?
ARE THESE THE WORTHLESS LANDS OVER WHICH WE SHOULD BE PROUD TO REIGN?
ARE THESE THE YOUNG KINGDOMS?
ALL I SEE ARE MUD, WOOD, AND ANIMALS.
ALL I SMELL ARE FILTH AND FEAR.
WHAT IS THERE FOR US HERE, CYMORIL?
WHAT IS THERE WE COULD NOT SEIZE OR BUY, CONQUER OR DESTROY?
WHAT IS THERE EVEN WORTH DESIRING...
...EXCEPT YOU?

ARE YOU WORRIED FOR HER, ELRIC?

HAVE YOU REASONS TO FEAR OUR QUEEN IS--?

SHE IS STILL ALIVE.

AND WILL REMAIN SO TILL YYRKOON GETS WHAT HE WANTS FROM ME.

YOUR LIFE, FOR HERS?

HE HAD A HUNDRED CHANCES TO KILL US IN IMRRYR.

IF HE CHOSE TO BRING HER HERE AND AWAIT ME IN THE RUINS OF--

?!

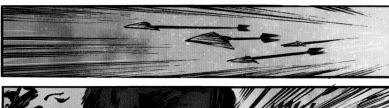

TCHAK! TCHAK! TCHAK!

SOLDIERS, I THINK WE'VE JUST CAUGHT DINNER!

HEY!

THAT'S...

...OUR BOAR!

THIS IS NO MERE DINNER NOW...

...BUT A FEAST!

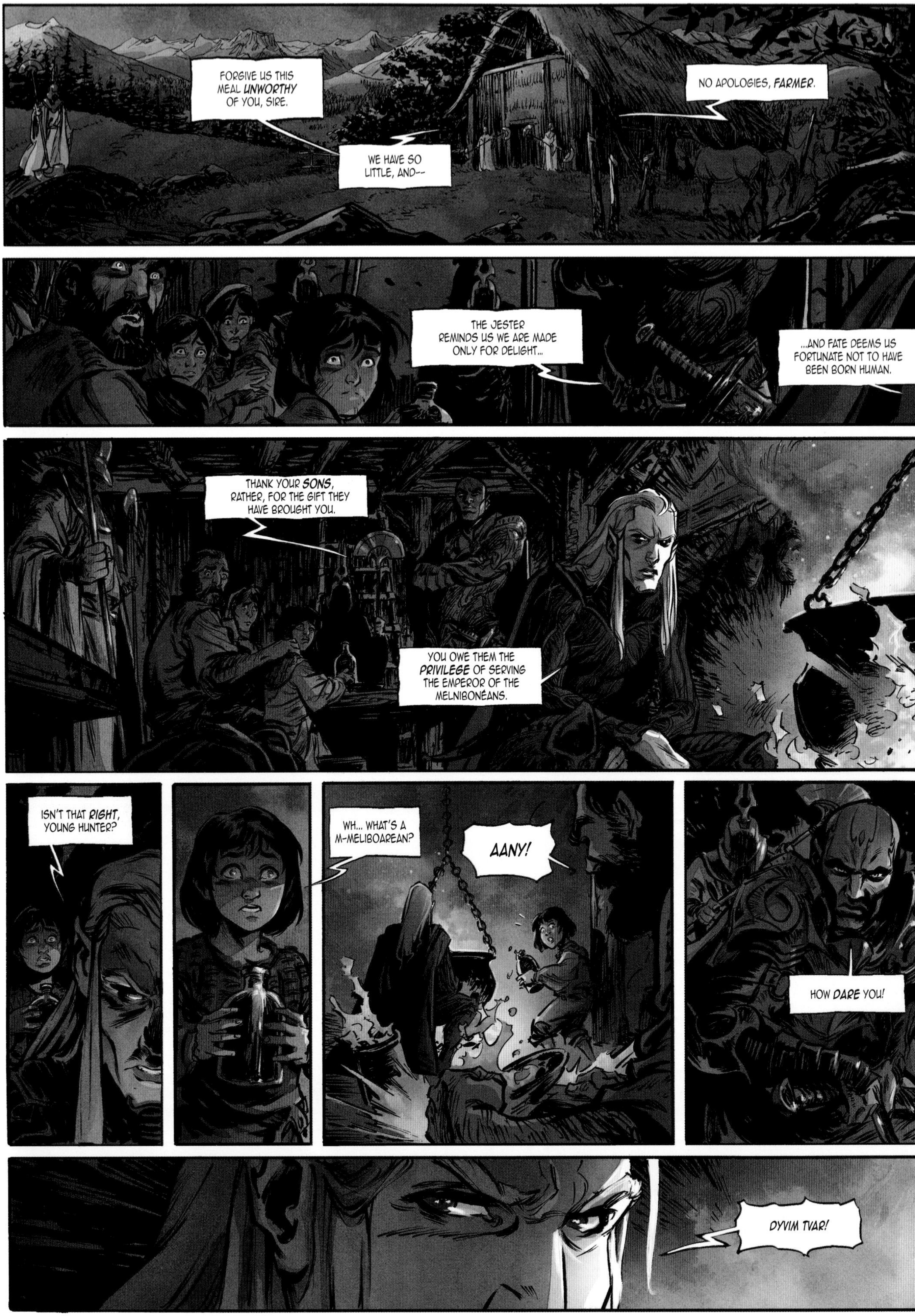

FORGIVE US THIS MEAL UNWORTHY OF YOU, SIRE.
WE HAVE SO LITTLE, AND--
NO APOLOGIES, FARMER.
THE JESTER REMINDS US WE ARE MADE ONLY FOR DELIGHT...
...AND FATE DEEMS US FORTUNATE NOT TO HAVE BEEN BORN HUMAN.
THANK YOUR SONS, RATHER, FOR THE GIFT THEY HAVE BROUGHT YOU.
YOU OWE THEM THE PRIVILEGE OF SERVING THE EMPEROR OF THE MELNIBONÉANS.
ISN'T THAT RIGHT, YOUNG HUNTER?
WH... WHAT'S A M-MELIBOAREAN?
AANY!
HOW DARE YOU!
DYVIM TVAR!

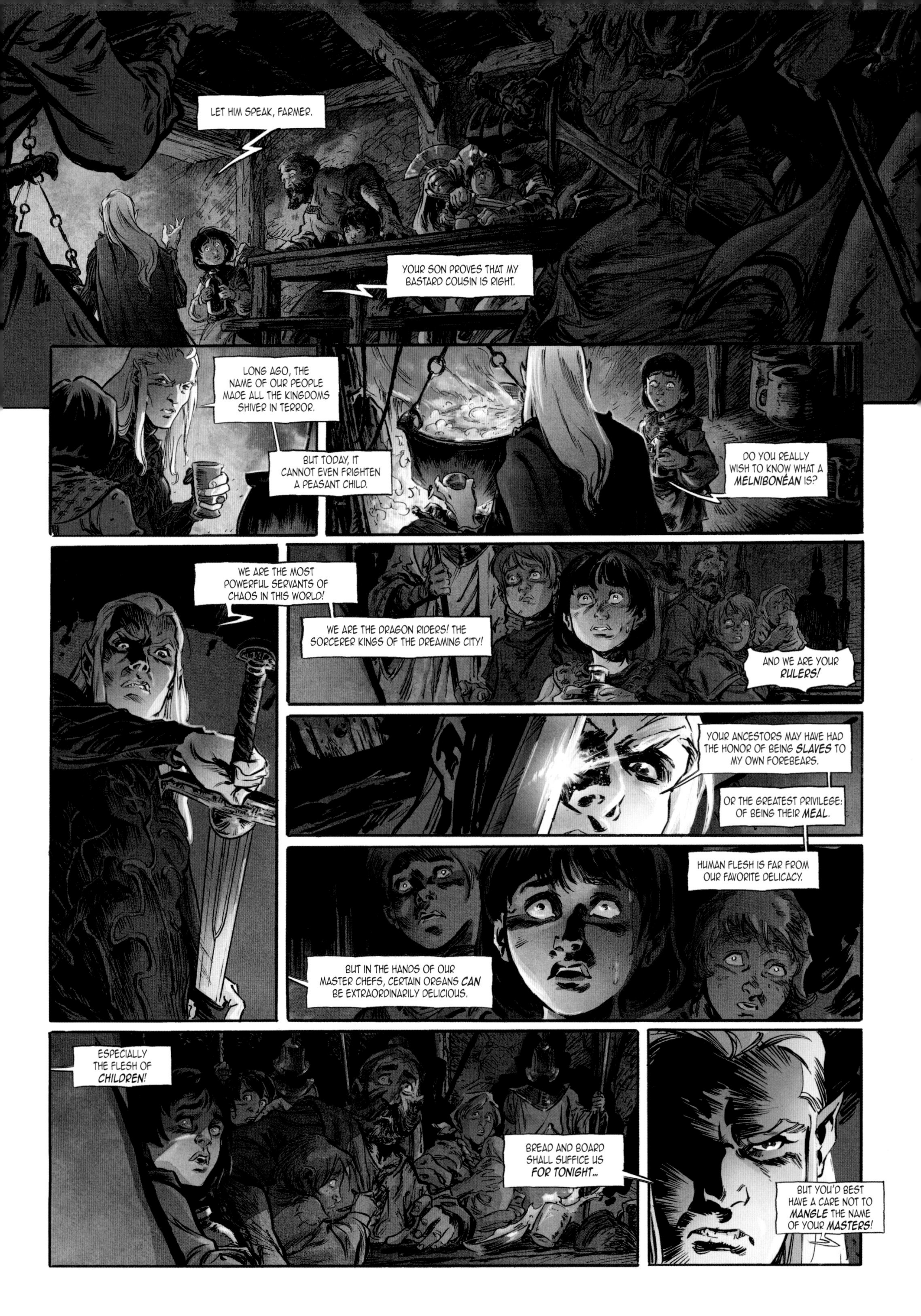
LET HIM SPEAK, FARMER.
YOUR SON PROVES THAT MY BASTARD COUSIN IS RIGHT.
LONG AGO, THE NAME OF OUR PEOPLE MADE ALL THE KINGDOMS SHIVER IN TERROR.
BUT TODAY, IT CANNOT EVEN FRIGHTEN A PEASANT CHILD.
DO YOU REALLY WISH TO KNOW WHAT A MELNIBONÉAN IS?
WE ARE THE MOST POWERFUL SERVANTS OF CHAOS IN THIS WORLD!
WE ARE THE DRAGON RIDERS! THE SORCERER KINGS OF THE DREAMING CITY!
AND WE ARE YOUR RULERS!
YOUR ANCESTORS MAY HAVE HAD THE HONOR OF BEING SLAVES TO MY OWN FOREBEARS.
OR THE GREATEST PRIVILEGE: OF BEING THEIR MEAL.
HUMAN FLESH IS FAR FROM OUR FAVORITE DELICACY.
BUT IN THE HANDS OF OUR MASTER CHEFS, CERTAIN ORGANS CAN BE EXTRAORDINARILY DELICIOUS.
ESPECIALLY THE FLESH OF CHILDREN!
BREAD AND BOARD SHALL SUFFICE US FOR TONIGHT...
BUT YOU'D BEST HAVE A CARE NOT TO MANGLE THE NAME OF YOUR MASTERS!

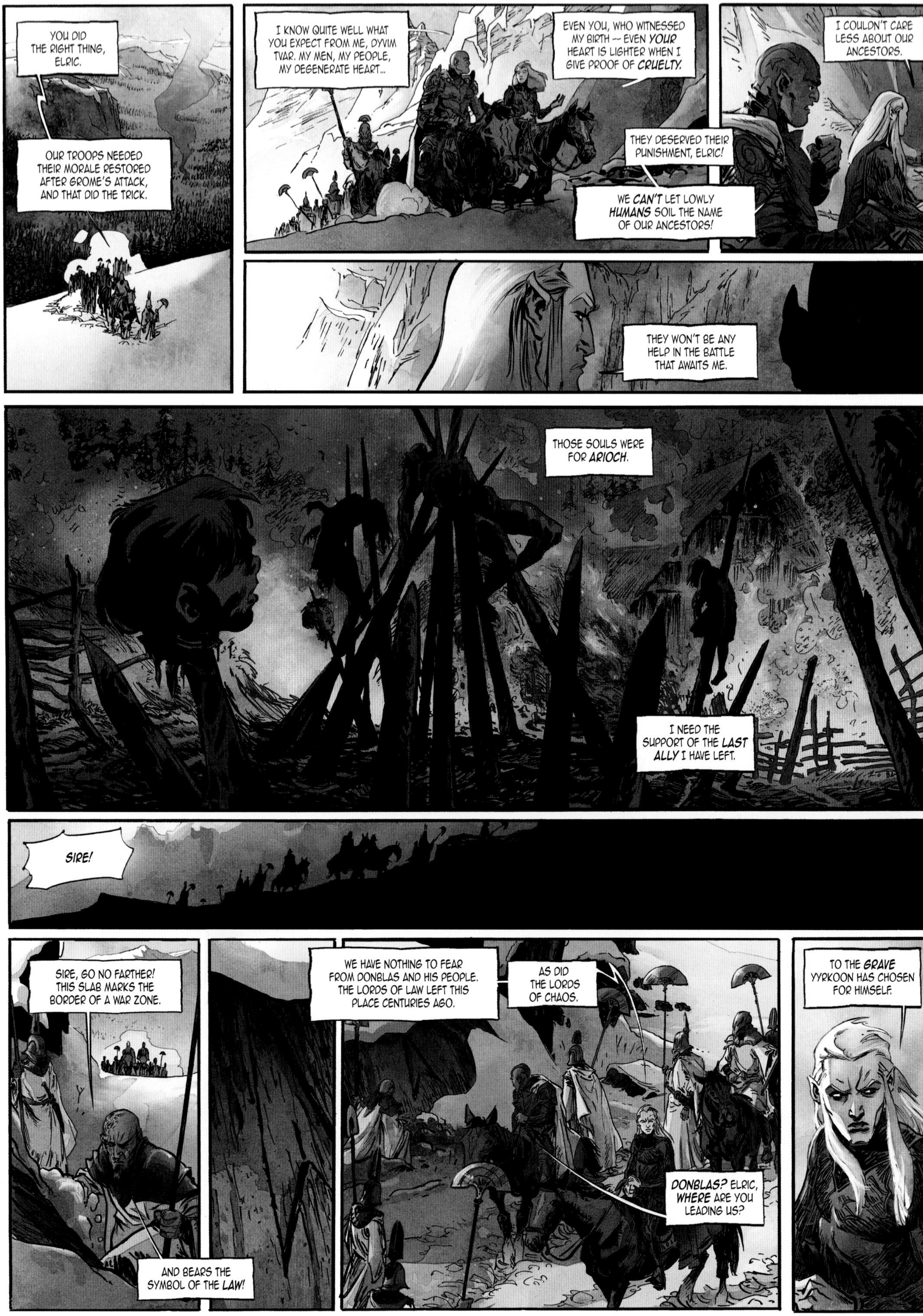
YOU DID THE RIGHT THING, ELRIC.
OUR TROOPS NEEDED THEIR MORALE RESTORED AFTER GROME'S ATTACK, AND THAT DID THE TRICK.
I KNOW QUITE WELL WHAT YOU EXPECT FROM ME, DYVIM TVAR. MY MEN, MY PEOPLE, MY DEGENERATE HEART...
EVEN YOU, WHO WITNESSED MY BIRTH -- EVEN YOUR HEART IS LIGHTER WHEN I GIVE PROOF OF CRUELTY.
THEY DESERVED THEIR PUNISHMENT, ELRIC!
WE CAN'T LET LOWLY HUMANS SOIL THE NAME OF OUR ANCESTORS!
I COULDN'T CARE LESS ABOUT OUR ANCESTORS.
THEY WON'T BE ANY HELP IN THE BATTLE THAT AWAITS ME.
THOSE SOULS WERE FOR ARIOCH.
I NEED THE SUPPORT OF THE LAST ALLY I HAVE LEFT.
SIRE!
SIRE, GO NO FARTHER! THIS SLAB MARKS THE BORDER OF A WAR ZONE.
AND BEARS THE SYMBOL OF THE LAW!
WE HAVE NOTHING TO FEAR FROM DONBLAS AND HIS PEOPLE. THE LORDS OF LAW LEFT THIS PLACE CENTURIES AGO.
AS DID THE LORDS OF CHAOS.
DONBLAS? ELRIC, WHERE ARE YOU LEADING US?
TO THE GRAVE YYRKOON HAS CHOSEN FOR HIMSELF.

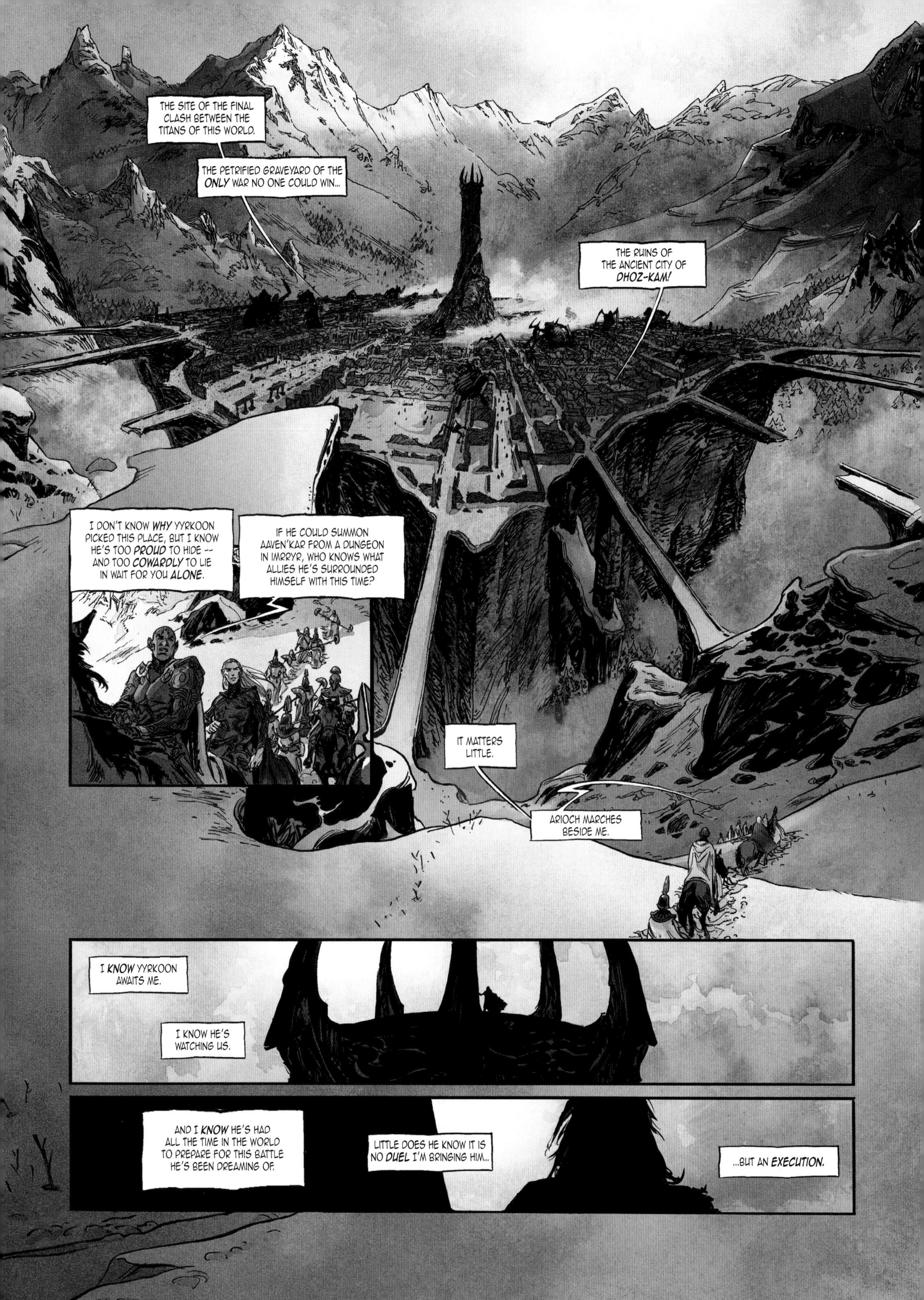

THE SITE OF THE FINAL CLASH BETWEEN THE TITANS OF THIS WORLD.
THE PETRIFIED GRAVEYARD OF THE ONLY WAR NO ONE COULD WIN...
THE RUINS OF THE ANCIENT CITY OF DHOZ-KAM!
I DON'T KNOW WHY YYRKOON PICKED THIS PLACE, BUT I KNOW HE'S TOO PROUD TO HIDE -- AND TOO COWARDLY TO LIE IN WAIT FOR YOU ALONE.
IF HE COULD SUMMON AAVEN'KAR FROM A DUNGEON IN IMRRYR, WHO KNOWS WHAT ALLIES HE'S SURROUNDED HIMSELF WITH THIS TIME?
IT MATTERS LITTLE.
ARIOCH MARCHES BESIDE ME.
I KNOW YYRKOON AWAITS ME.
I KNOW HE'S WATCHING US.
AND I KNOW HE'S HAD ALL THE TIME IN THE WORLD TO PREPARE FOR THIS BATTLE HE'S BEEN DREAMING OF.
LITTLE DOES HE KNOW IT IS NO DUEL I'M BRINGING HIM...
...BUT AN EXECUTION.

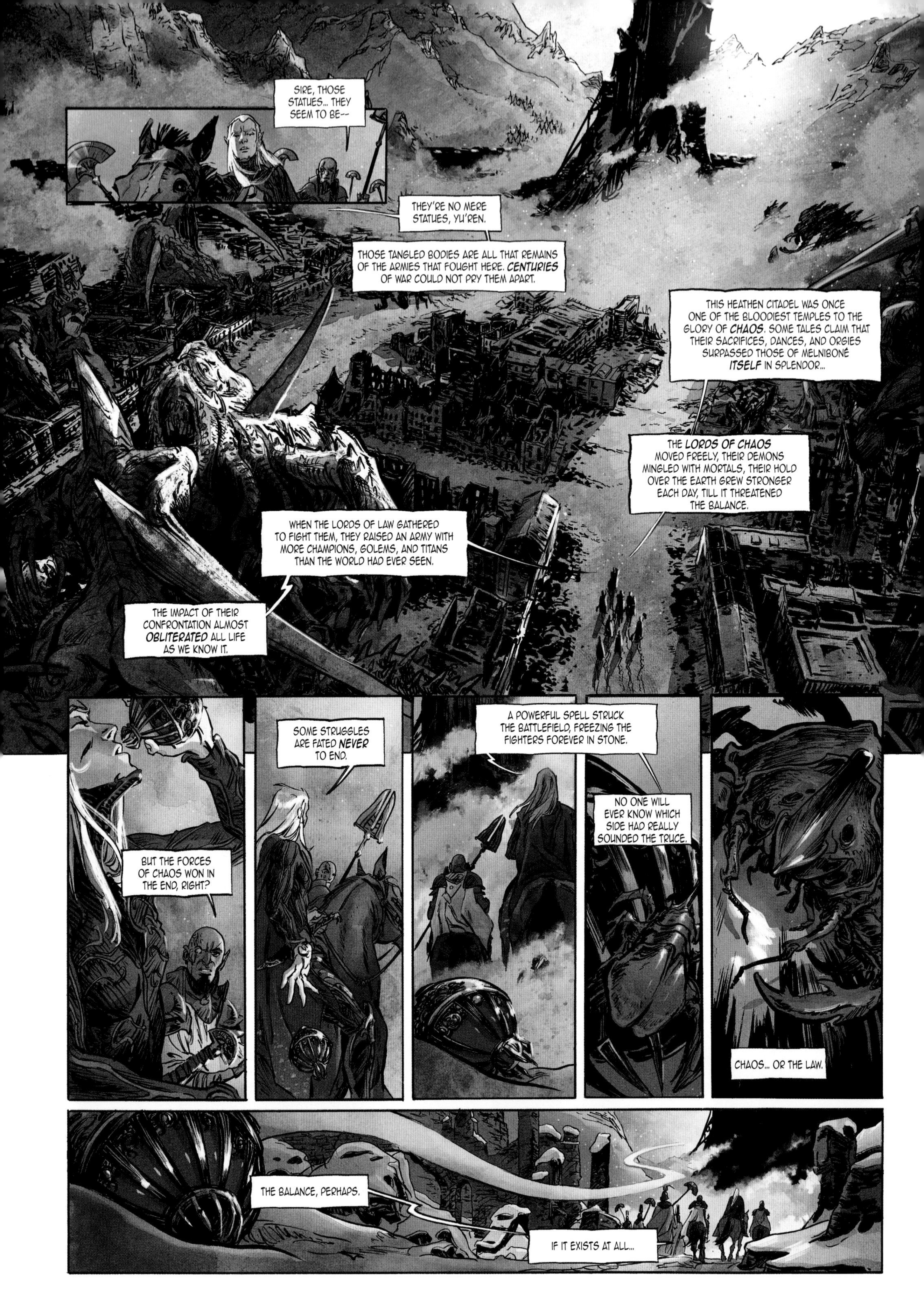
SIRE, THOSE STATUES... THEY SEEM TO BE--
THEY'RE NO MERE STATUES, YU'REN.
THOSE TANGLED BODIES ARE ALL THAT REMAINS OF THE ARMIES THAT FOUGHT HERE. CENTURIES OF WAR COULD NOT PRY THEM APART.
THIS HEATHEN CITADEL WAS ONCE ONE OF THE BLOODIEST TEMPLES TO THE GLORY OF CHAOS. SOME TALES CLAIM THAT THEIR SACRIFICES, DANCES, AND ORGIES SURPASSED THOSE OF MELNIBONÉ ITSELF IN SPLENDOR...
THE LORDS OF CHAOS MOVED FREELY, THEIR DEMONS MINGLED WITH MORTALS, THEIR HOLD OVER THE EARTH GREW STRONGER EACH DAY, TILL IT THREATENED THE BALANCE.
WHEN THE LORDS OF LAW GATHERED TO FIGHT THEM, THEY RAISED AN ARMY WITH MORE CHAMPIONS, GOLEMS, AND TITANS THAN THE WORLD HAD EVER SEEN.
THE IMPACT OF THEIR CONFRONTATION ALMOST OBLITERATED ALL LIFE AS WE KNOW IT.
BUT THE FORCES OF CHAOS WON IN THE END, RIGHT?
SOME STRUGGLES ARE FATED NEVER TO END.
A POWERFUL SPELL STRUCK THE BATTLEFIELD, FREEZING THE FIGHTERS FOREVER IN STONE.
NO ONE WILL EVER KNOW WHICH SIDE HAD REALLY SOUNDED THE TRUCE.
CHAOS... OR THE LAW.
THE BALANCE, PERHAPS.
IF IT EXISTS AT ALL...

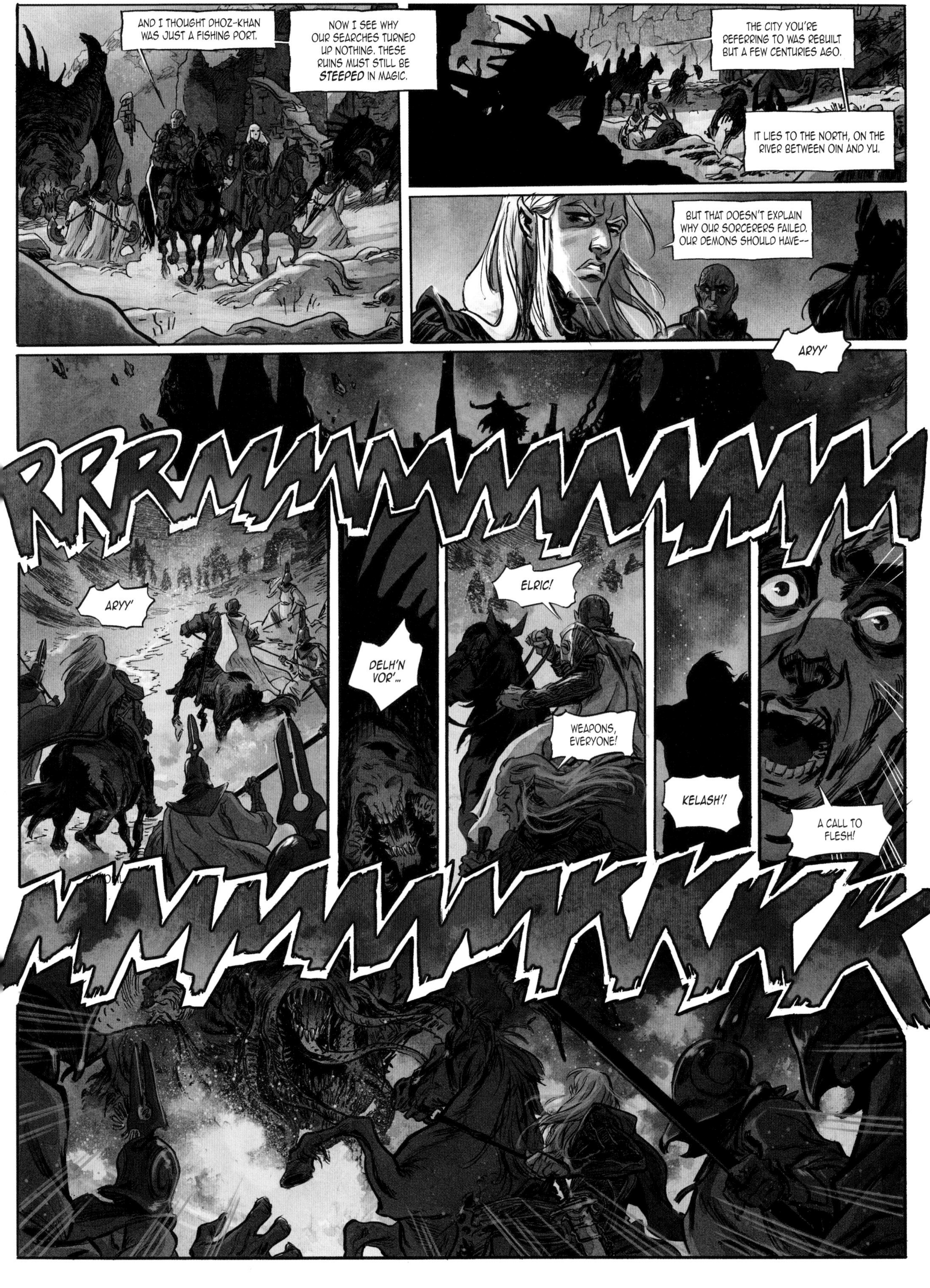
AND I THOUGHT DHOZ-KHAN WAS JUST A FISHING PORT.
NOW I SEE WHY OUR SEARCHES TURNED UP NOTHING. THESE RUINS MUST STILL BE STEEPED IN MAGIC.
THE CITY YOU'RE REFERRING TO WAS REBUILT BUT A FEW CENTURIES AGO.
IT LIES TO THE NORTH, ON THE RIVER BETWEEN OIN AND YU.
BUT THAT DOESN'T EXPLAIN WHY OUR SORCERERS FAILED. OUR DEMONS SHOULD HAVE--
ARYY'
RRRMMMMMMMMMMMMMMMMMMMMKKKK
ARYY'
DELH'N VOR'...
ELRIC!
WEAPONS, EVERYONE!
KELASH'!
A CALL TO FLESH!

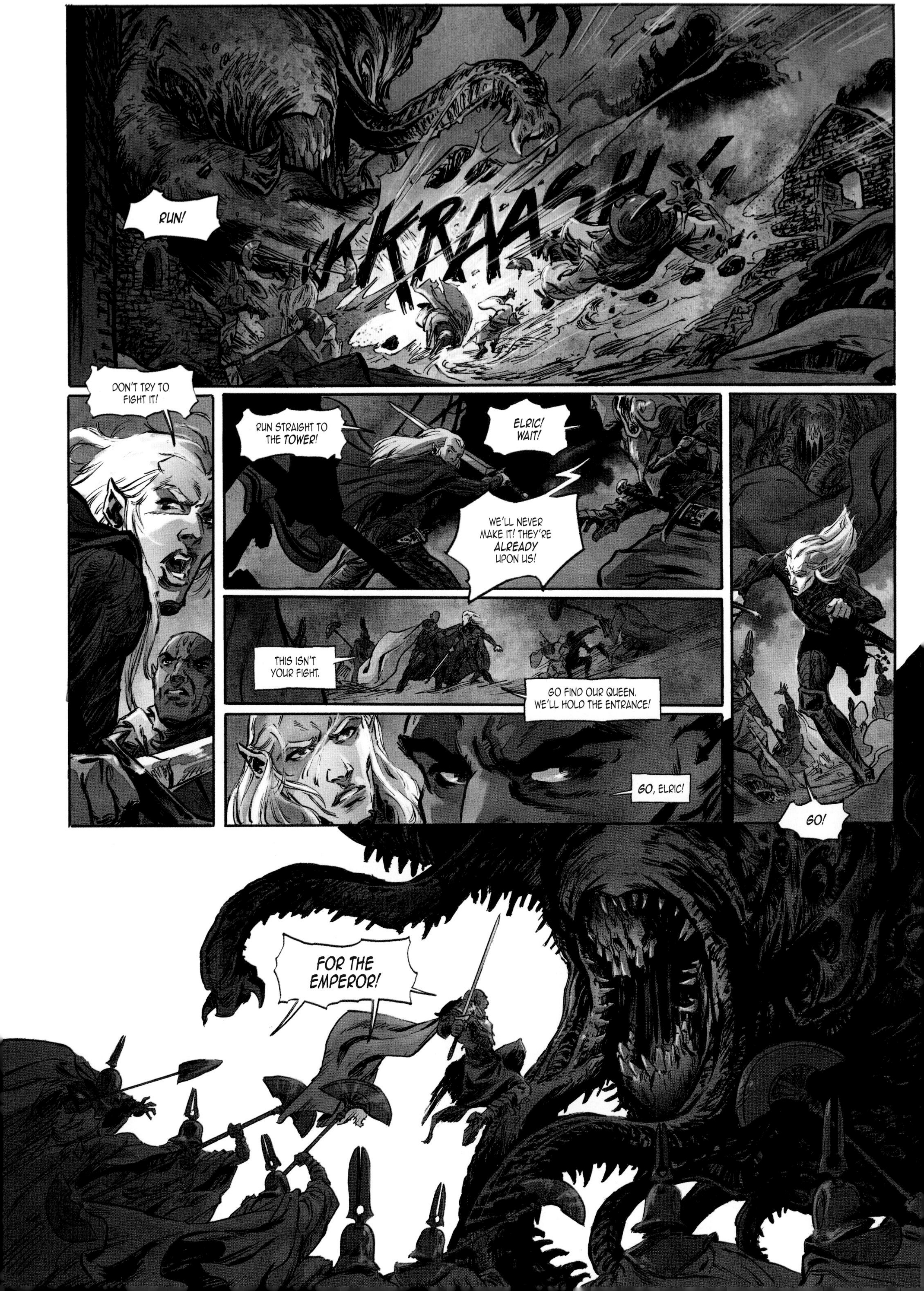
RUN!
KKRAASH!!
DON'T TRY TO FIGHT IT!
RUN STRAIGHT TO THE TOWER!
ELRIC! WAIT!
WE'LL NEVER MAKE IT! THEY'RE ALREADY UPON US!
THIS ISN'T YOUR FIGHT.
GO FIND OUR QUEEN. WE'LL HOLD THE ENTRANCE!
GO, ELRIC!
GO!
FOR THE EMPEROR!

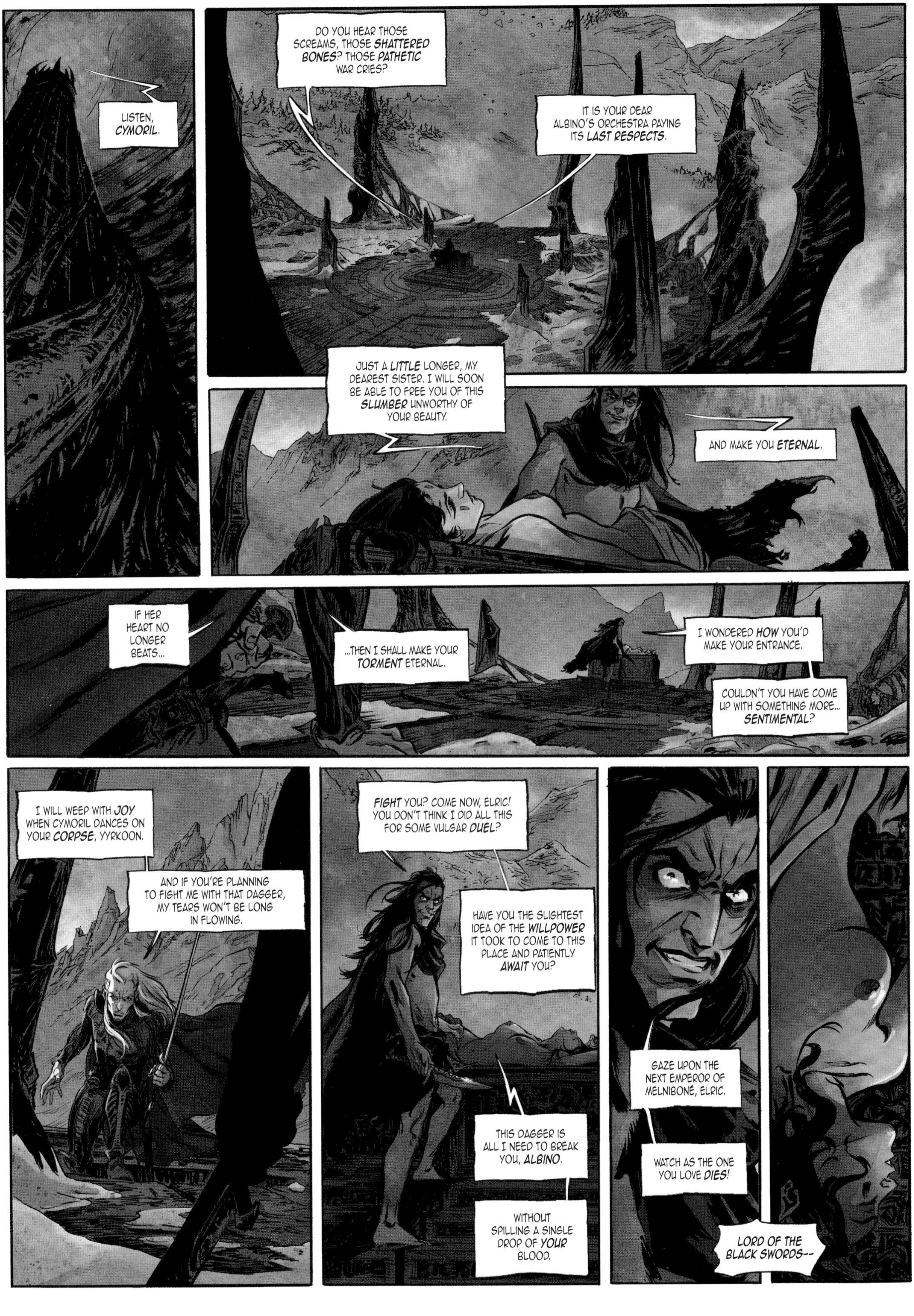
LISTEN, CYMORIL.
DO YOU HEAR THOSE SCREAMS, THOSE SHATTERED BONES? THOSE PATHETIC WAR CRIES?
IT IS YOUR DEAR ALBINO'S ORCHESTRA PAYING ITS LAST RESPECTS.
JUST A LITTLE LONGER, MY DEAREST SISTER. I WILL SOON BE ABLE TO FREE YOU OF THIS SLUMBER UNWORTHY OF YOUR BEAUTY.
AND MAKE YOU ETERNAL.
IF HER HEART NO LONGER BEATS...
...THEN I SHALL MAKE YOUR TORMENT ETERNAL.
I WONDERED HOW YOU'D MAKE YOUR ENTRANCE.
COULDN'T YOU HAVE COME UP WITH SOMETHING MORE... SENTIMENTAL?
I WILL WEEP WITH JOY WHEN CYMORIL DANCES ON YOUR CORPSE, YYRKOON.
AND IF YOU'RE PLANNING TO FIGHT ME WITH THAT DAGGER, MY TEARS WON'T BE LONG IN FLOWING.
FIGHT YOU? COME NOW, ELRIC! YOU DON'T THINK I DID ALL THIS FOR SOME VULGAR DUEL?
HAVE YOU THE SLIGHTEST IDEA OF THE WILLPOWER IT TOOK TO COME TO THIS PLACE AND PATIENTLY AWAIT YOU?
THIS DAGGER IS ALL I NEED TO BREAK YOU, ALBINO.
WITHOUT SPILLING A SINGLE DROP OF YOUR BLOOD.
GAZE UPON THE NEXT EMPEROR OF MELNIBONÉ, ELRIC.
WATCH AS THE ONE YOU LOVE DIES!
LORD OF THE BLACK SWORDS--

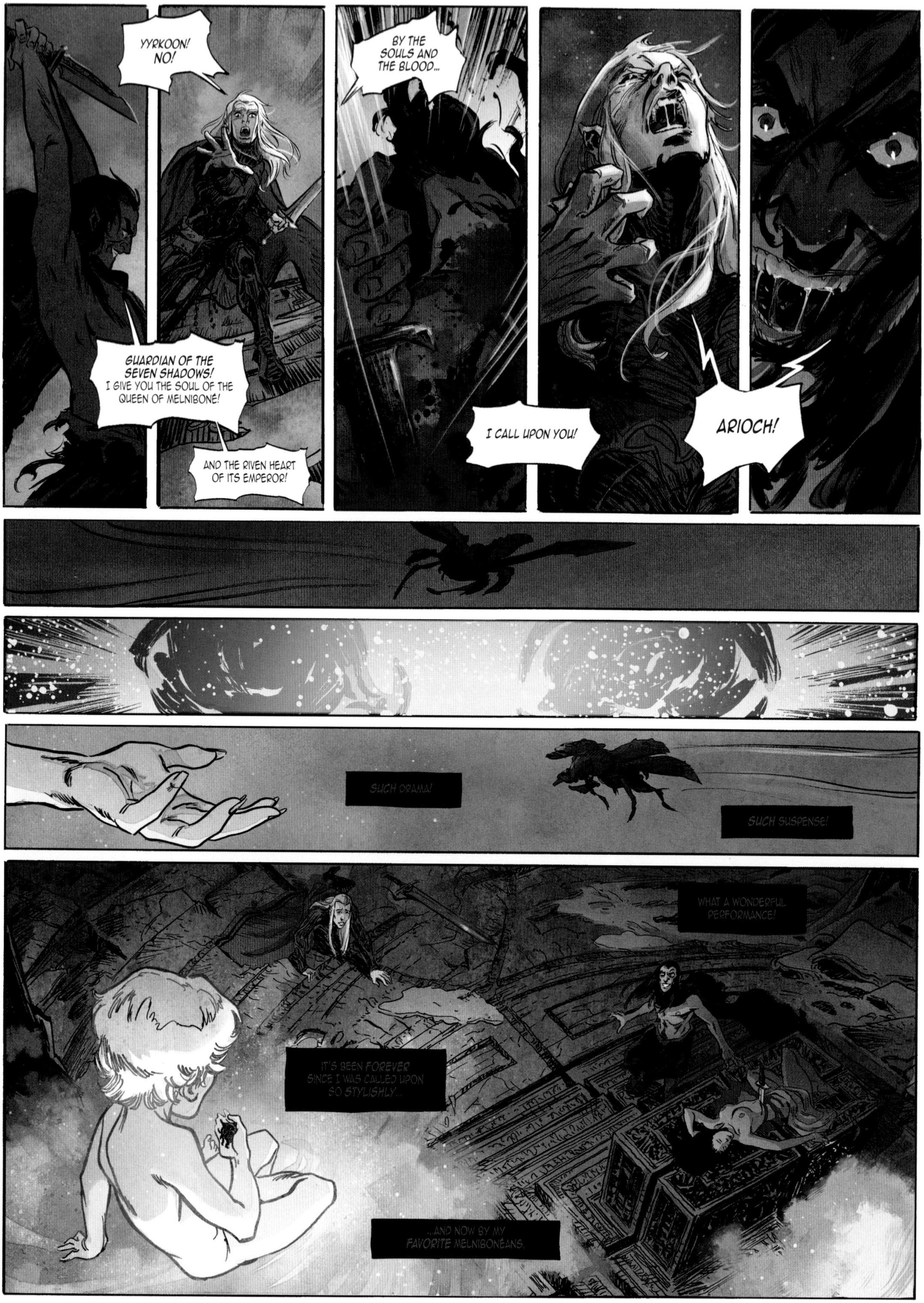
YYRKOON! NO!
GUARDIAN OF THE SEVEN SHADOWS! I GIVE YOU THE SOUL OF THE QUEEN OF MELNIBONÉ!
AND THE RIVEN HEART OF ITS EMPEROR!
BY THE SOULS AND THE BLOOD...
I CALL UPON YOU!
ARIOCH!
SUCH DRAMA!
SUCH SUSPENSE!
WHAT A WONDERFUL PERFORMANCE!
IT'S BEEN FOREVER SINCE I WAS CALLED UPON SO STYLISHLY...
...AND NOW BY MY FAVORITE MELNIBONÉANS.

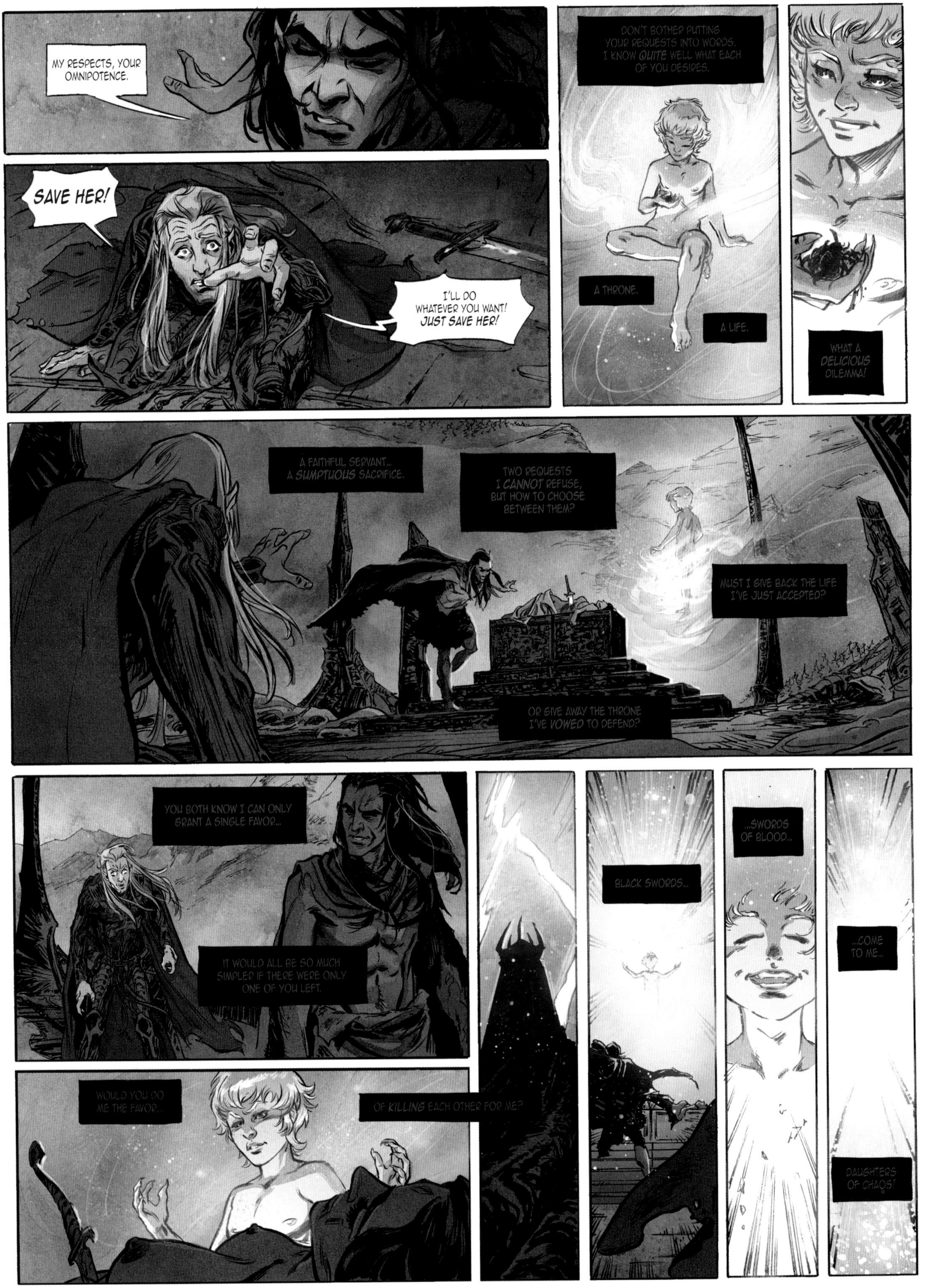
MY RESPECTS, YOUR OMNIPOTENCE.
SAVE HER!
I'LL DO WHATEVER YOU WANT! JUST SAVE HER!
DON'T BOTHER PUTTING YOUR REQUESTS INTO WORDS. I KNOW QUITE WELL WHAT EACH OF YOU DESIRES.
A THRONE.
A LIFE.
WHAT A DELICIOUS DILEMMA!
A FAITHFUL SERVANT... A SUMPTUOUS SACRIFICE.
TWO REQUESTS I CANNOT REFUSE, BUT HOW TO CHOOSE BETWEEN THEM?
MUST I GIVE BACK THE LIFE I'VE JUST ACCEPTED?
OR GIVE AWAY THE THRONE I'VE VOWED TO DEFEND?
YOU BOTH KNOW I CAN ONLY GRANT A SINGLE FAVOR...
IT WOULD ALL BE SO MUCH SIMPLER IF THERE WERE ONLY ONE OF YOU LEFT.
WOULD YOU DO ME THE FAVOR...
OF KILLING EACH OTHER FOR ME?
BLACK SWORDS...
...SWORDS OF BLOOD...
...COME TO ME...
DAUGHTERS OF CHAOS!

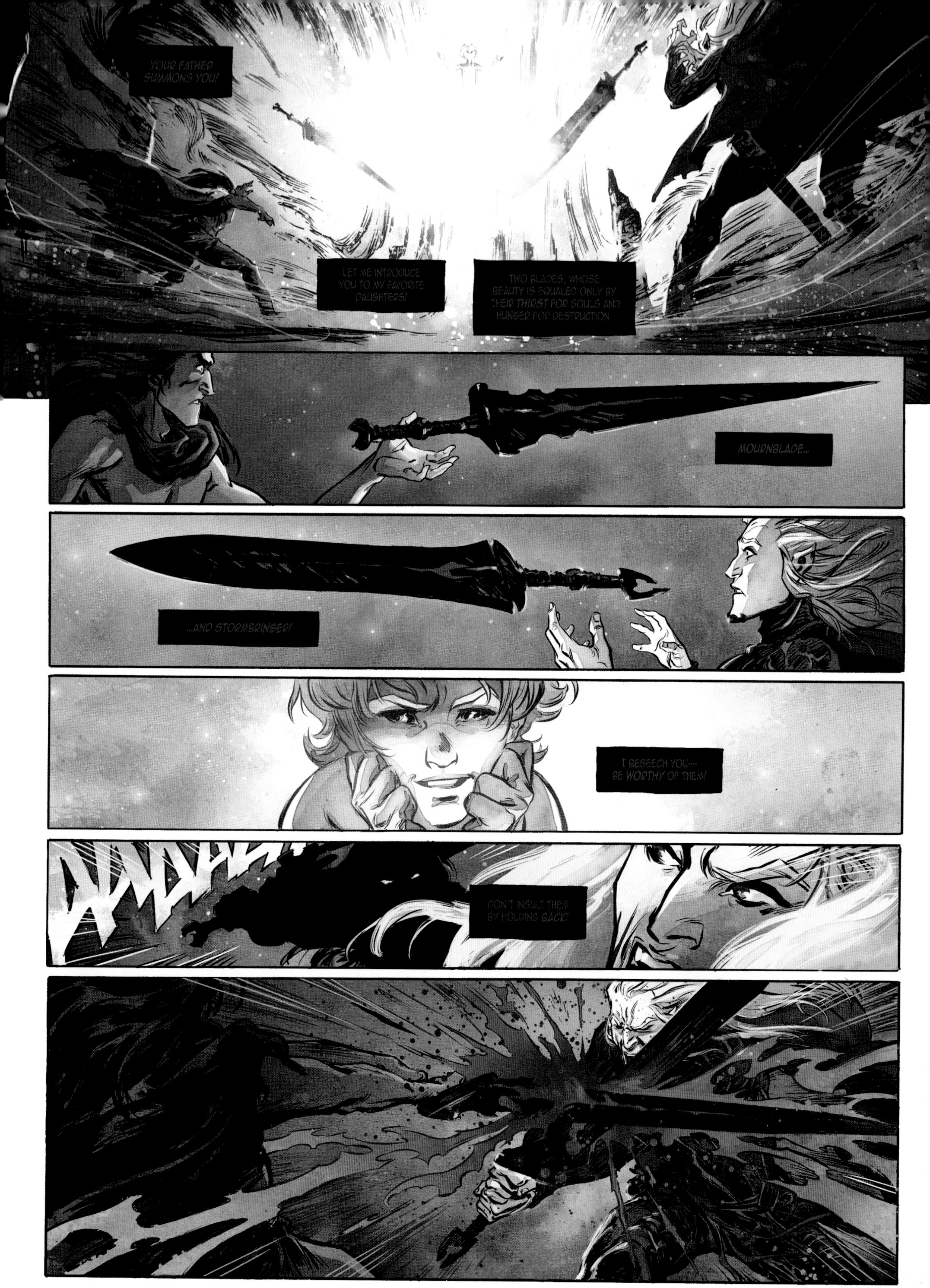
YOUR FATHER SUMMONS YOU!
LET ME INTRODUCE YOU TO MY FAVORITE DAUGHTERS!
TWO BLADES, WHOSE BEAUTY IS EQUALED ONLY BY THEIR THIRST FOR SOULS AND HUNGER FOR DESTRUCTION.
MOURNBLADE...
...AND STORMBRINGER!
I BESEECH YOU-- BE WORTHY OF THEM!
DON'T INSULT THEM BY HOLDING BACK!

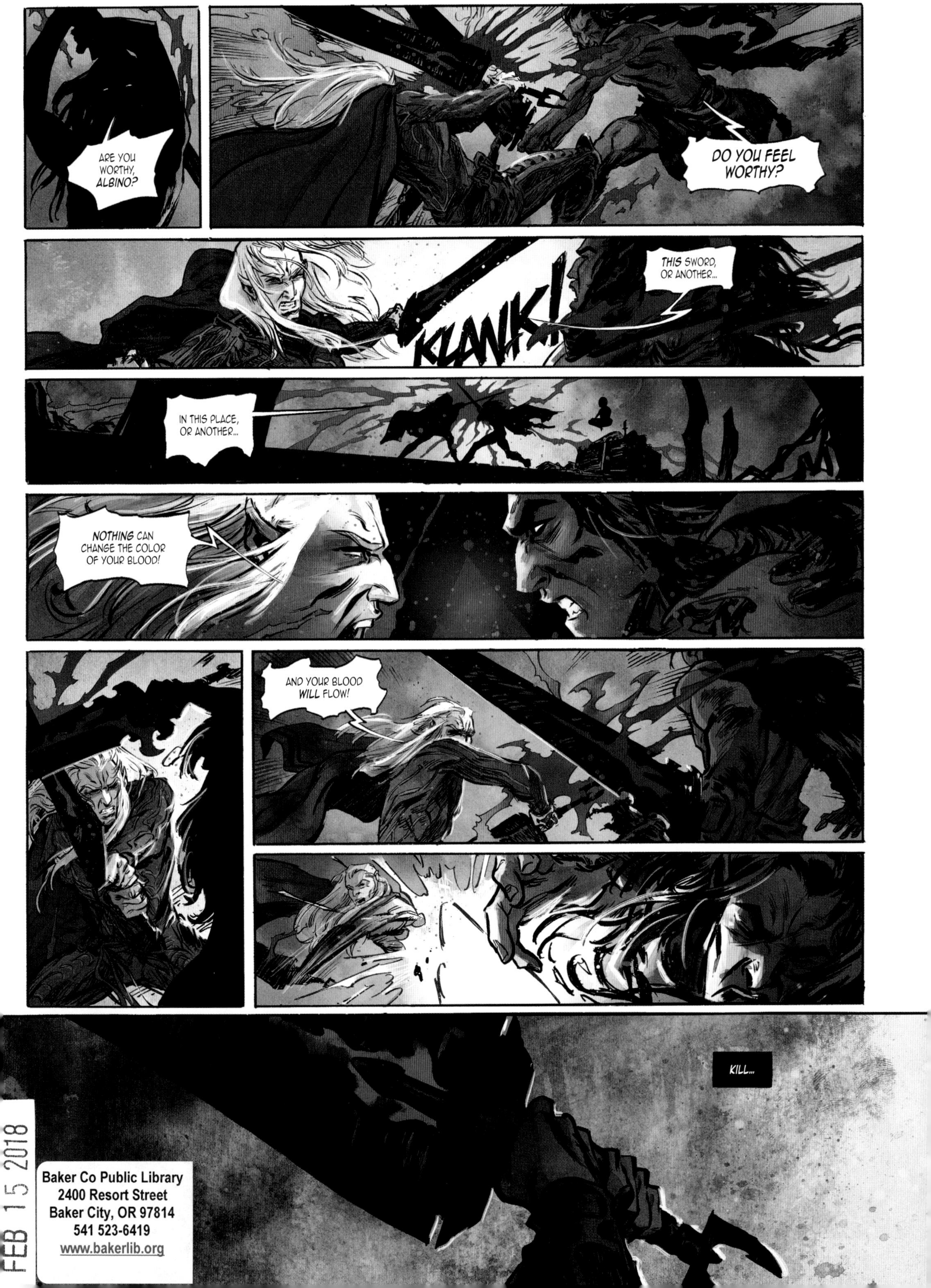
ARE YOU WORTHY, ALBINO?
DO YOU FEEL WORTHY?
THIS SWORD, OR ANOTHER...
KLANK!!
IN THIS PLACE, OR ANOTHER...
NOTHING CAN CHANGE THE COLOR OF YOUR BLOOD!
AND YOUR BLOOD WILL FLOW!
KILL...

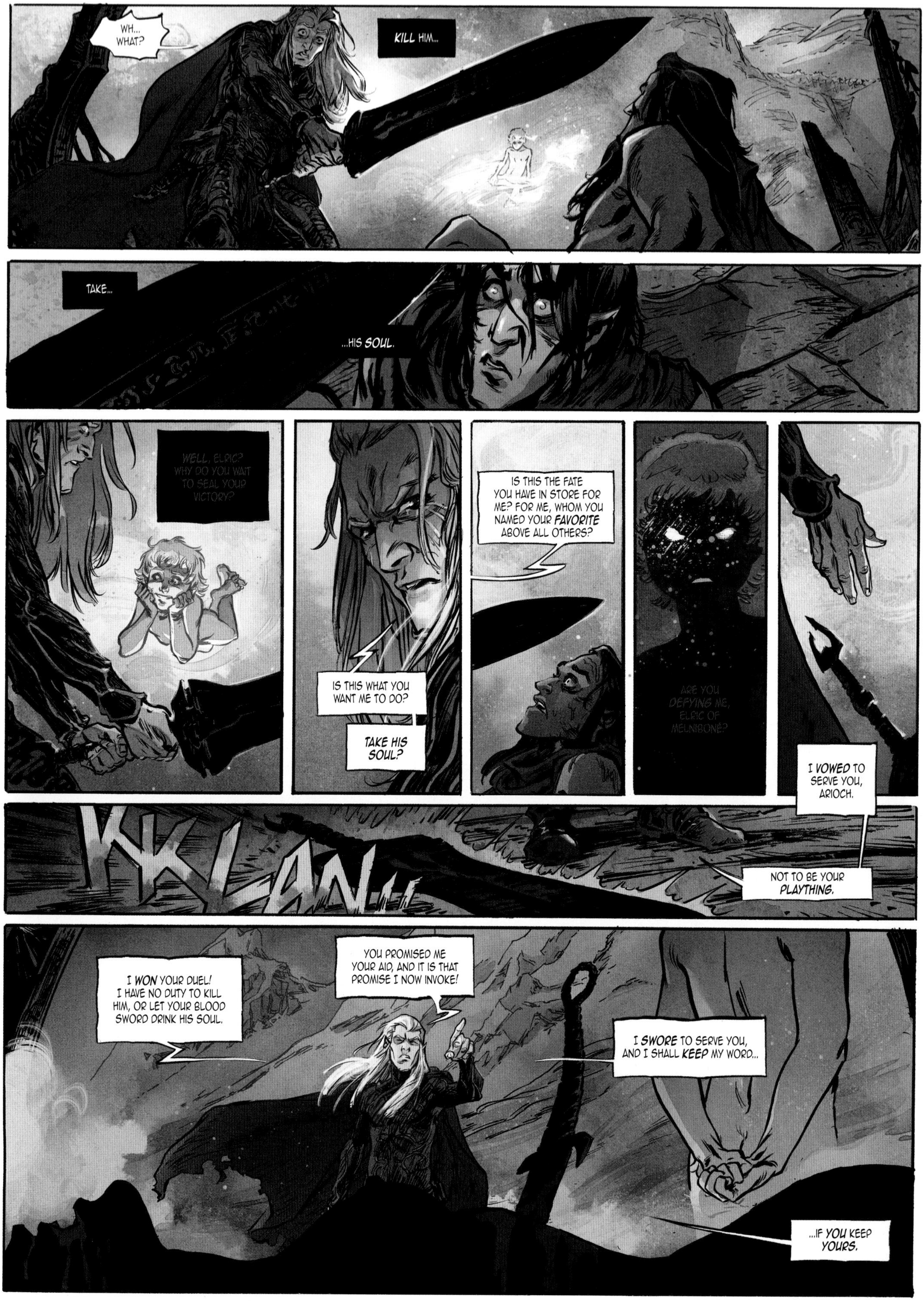

WH... WHAT?
KILL HIM...
TAKE...
...HIS SOUL.
WELL, ELRIC? WHY DO YOU WAIT TO SEAL YOUR VICTORY?
IS THIS WHAT YOU WANT ME TO DO?
TAKE HIS SOUL?
IS THIS THE FATE YOU HAVE IN STORE FOR ME? FOR ME, WHOM YOU NAMED YOUR FAVORITE ABOVE ALL OTHERS?
ARE YOU DEFYING ME, ELRIC OF MELNIBONÉ?
I VOWED TO SERVE YOU, ARIOCH.
NOT TO BE YOUR PLAYTHING.
I WON YOUR DUEL! I HAVE NO DUTY TO KILL HIM, OR LET YOUR BLOOD SWORD DRINK HIS SOUL.
YOU PROMISED ME YOUR AID, AND IT IS THAT PROMISE I NOW INVOKE!
I SWORE TO SERVE YOU, AND I SHALL KEEP MY WORD...
...IF YOU KEEP YOURS.

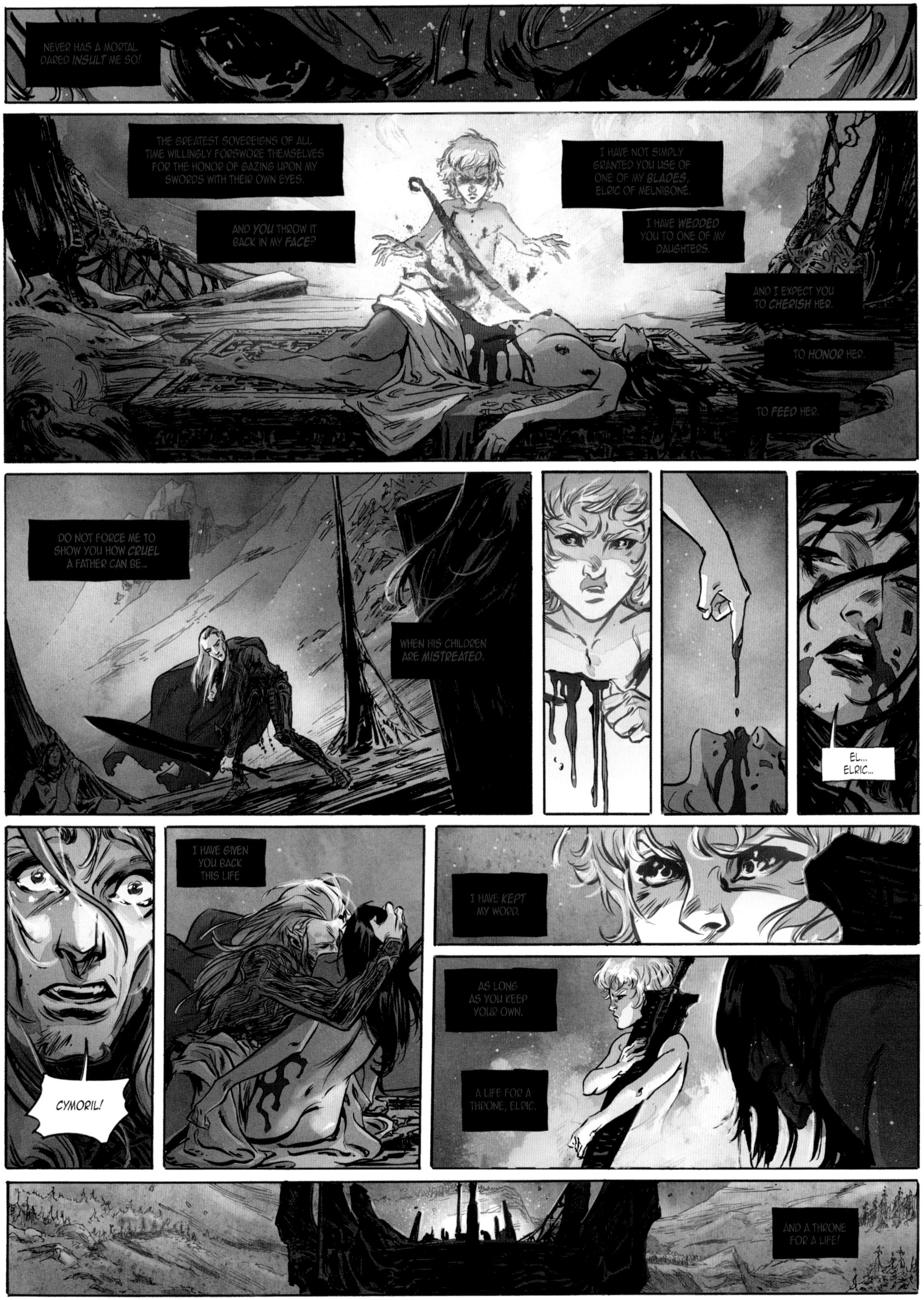
NEVER HAS A MORTAL DARED INSULT ME SO!
THE GREATEST SOVEREIGNS OF ALL TIME WILLINGLY FORSWORE THEMSELVES FOR THE HONOR OF GAZING UPON MY SWORDS WITH THEIR OWN EYES.
AND YOU THROW IT BACK IN MY FACE?
I HAVE NOT SIMPLY GRANTED YOU USE OF ONE OF MY BLADES, ELRIC OF MELNIBONÉ.
I HAVE WEDDED YOU TO ONE OF MY DAUGHTERS.
AND I EXPECT YOU TO CHERISH HER.
TO HONOR HER.
TO FEED HER.
DO NOT FORCE ME TO SHOW YOU HOW CRUEL A FATHER CAN BE...
WHEN HIS CHILDREN ARE MISTREATED.
EL... ELRIC...
CYMORIL!
I HAVE GIVEN YOU BACK THIS LIFE
I HAVE KEPT MY WORD.
AS LONG AS YOU KEEP YOUR OWN.
A LIFE FOR A THRONE, ELRIC.
AND A THRONE FOR A LIFE!

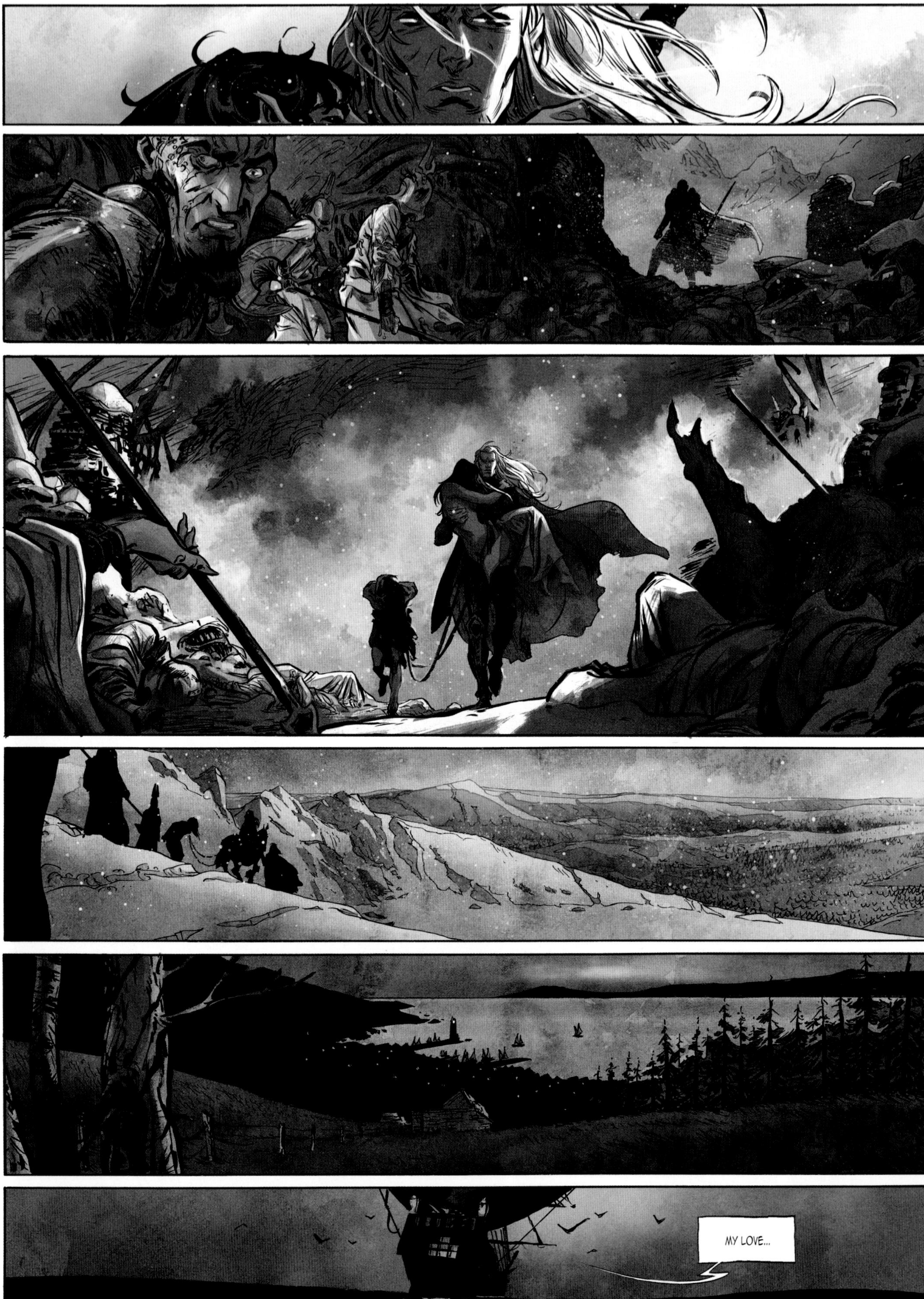
MY LOVE...

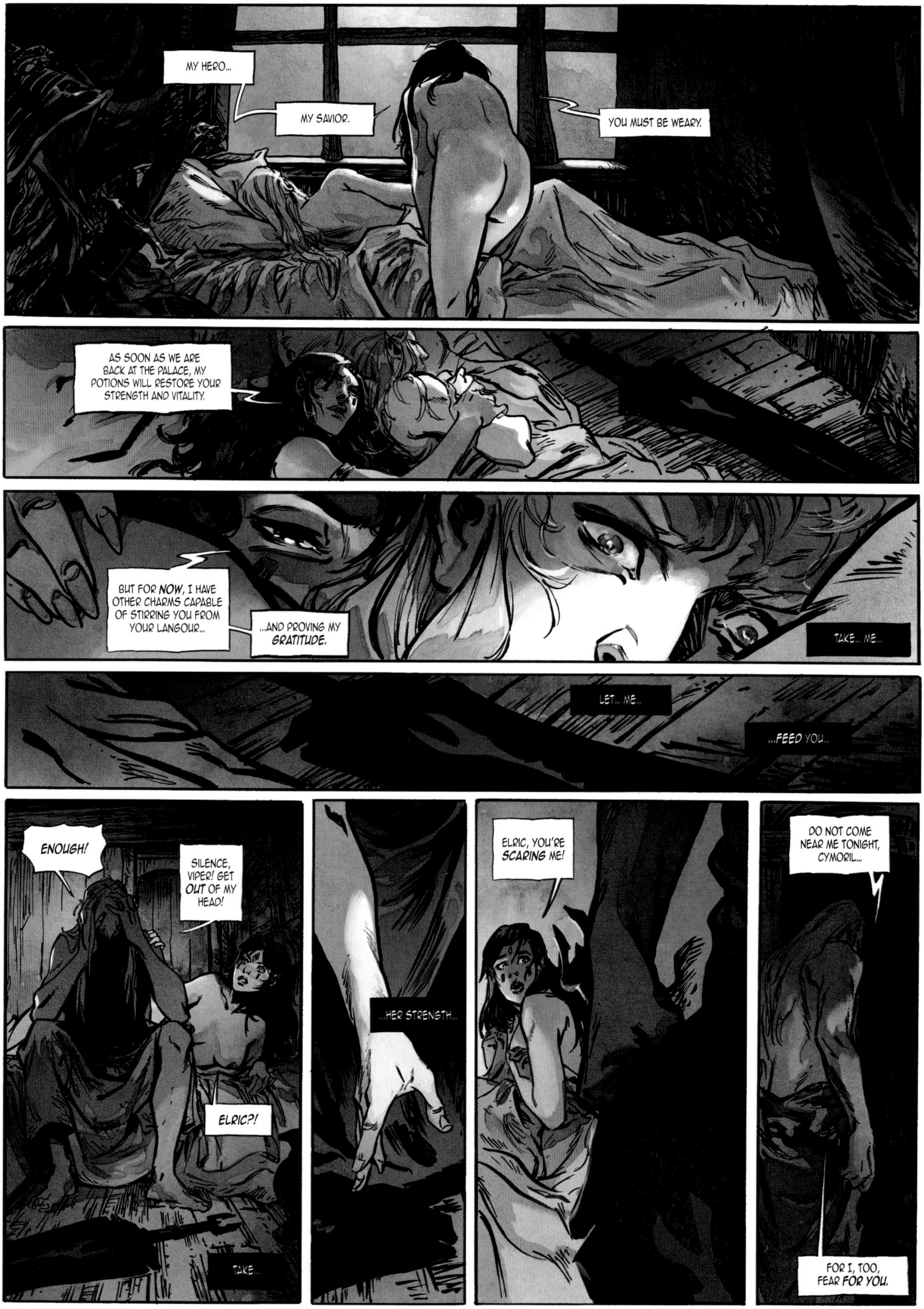
MY HERO...
MY SAVIOR.
YOU MUST BE WEARY.
AS SOON AS WE ARE BACK AT THE PALACE, MY POTIONS WILL RESTORE YOUR STRENGTH AND VITALITY.
BUT FOR NOW, I HAVE OTHER CHARMS CAPABLE OF STIRRING YOU FROM YOUR LANGOUR...
...AND PROVING MY GRATITUDE.
TAKE... ME...
LET... ME...
...FEED YOU...
ENOUGH!
SILENCE, VIPER! GET OUT OF MY HEAD!
ELRIC?!
TAKE...
...HER STRENGTH...
ELRIC, YOU'RE SCARING ME!
DO NOT COME NEAR ME TONIGHT, CYMORIL...
FOR I, TOO, FEAR FOR YOU.

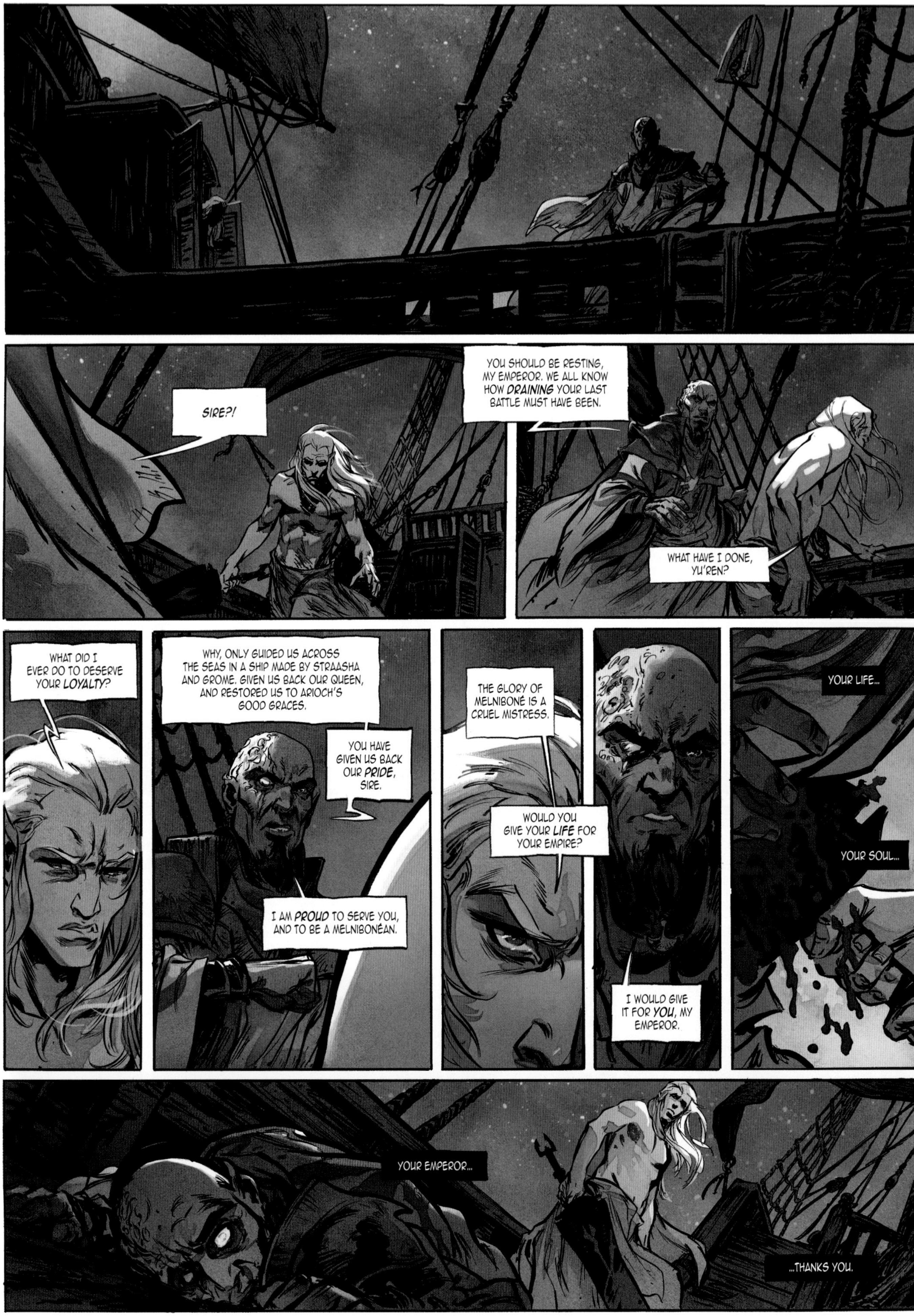
SIRE?!
YOU SHOULD BE RESTING, MY EMPEROR. WE ALL KNOW HOW *DRAINING* YOUR LAST BATTLE MUST HAVE BEEN.
WHAT HAVE I DONE, YU'REN?
WHAT DID I EVER DO TO DESERVE YOUR *LOYALTY*?
WHY, ONLY GUIDED US ACROSS THE SEAS IN A SHIP MADE BY STRAASHA AND GROME. GIVEN US BACK OUR QUEEN, AND RESTORED US TO ARIOCH'S GOOD GRACES.
YOU HAVE GIVEN US BACK OUR *PRIDE*, SIRE.
I AM *PROUD* TO SERVE YOU, AND TO BE A MELNIBONÉAN.
THE GLORY OF MELNIBONÉ IS A CRUEL MISTRESS.
WOULD YOU GIVE YOUR *LIFE* FOR YOUR EMPIRE?
I WOULD GIVE IT FOR *YOU*, MY EMPEROR.
YOUR LIFE...
YOUR SOUL...
YOUR EMPEROR...
...THANKS YOU.

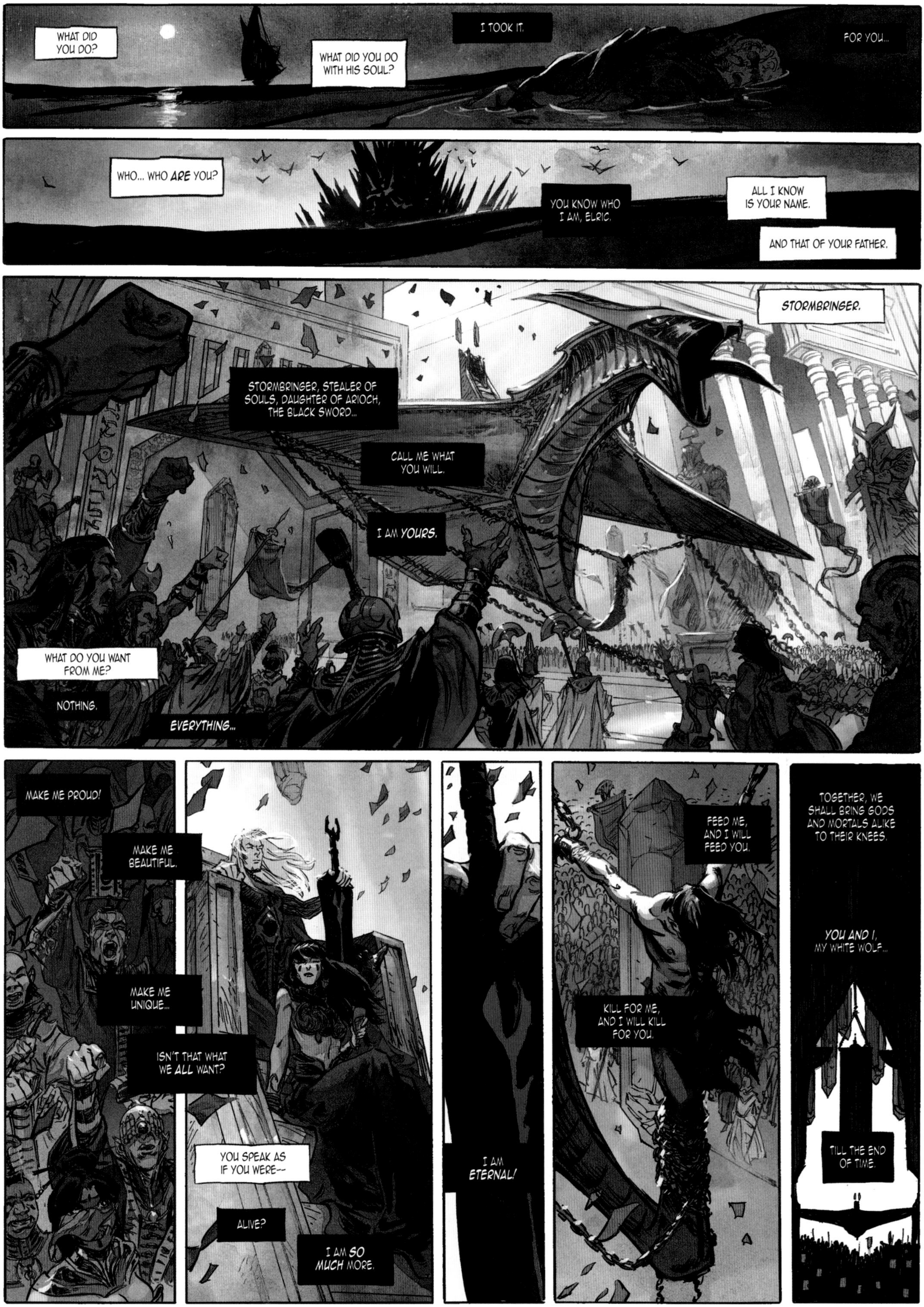
WHAT DID YOU DO?
WHAT DID YOU DO WITH HIS SOUL?
I TOOK IT.
FOR YOU...
WHO... WHO ARE YOU?
YOU KNOW WHO I AM, ELRIC.
ALL I KNOW IS YOUR NAME.
AND THAT OF YOUR FATHER.
STORMBRINGER.
STORMBRINGER, STEALER OF SOULS, DAUGHTER OF ARIOCH, THE BLACK SWORD...
CALL ME WHAT YOU WILL.
I AM YOURS.
WHAT DO YOU WANT FROM ME?
NOTHING.
EVERYTHING...
MAKE ME PROUD!
MAKE ME BEAUTIFUL.
MAKE ME UNIQUE...
ISN'T THAT WHAT WE ALL WANT?
YOU SPEAK AS IF YOU WERE--
ALIVE?
I AM SO MUCH MORE.
I AM ETERNAL!
FEED ME, AND I WILL FEED YOU.
KILL FOR ME, AND I WILL KILL FOR YOU.
TOGETHER, WE SHALL BRING GODS AND MORTALS ALIKE TO THEIR KNEES.
YOU AND I, MY WHITE WOLF...
TILL THE END OF TIME.

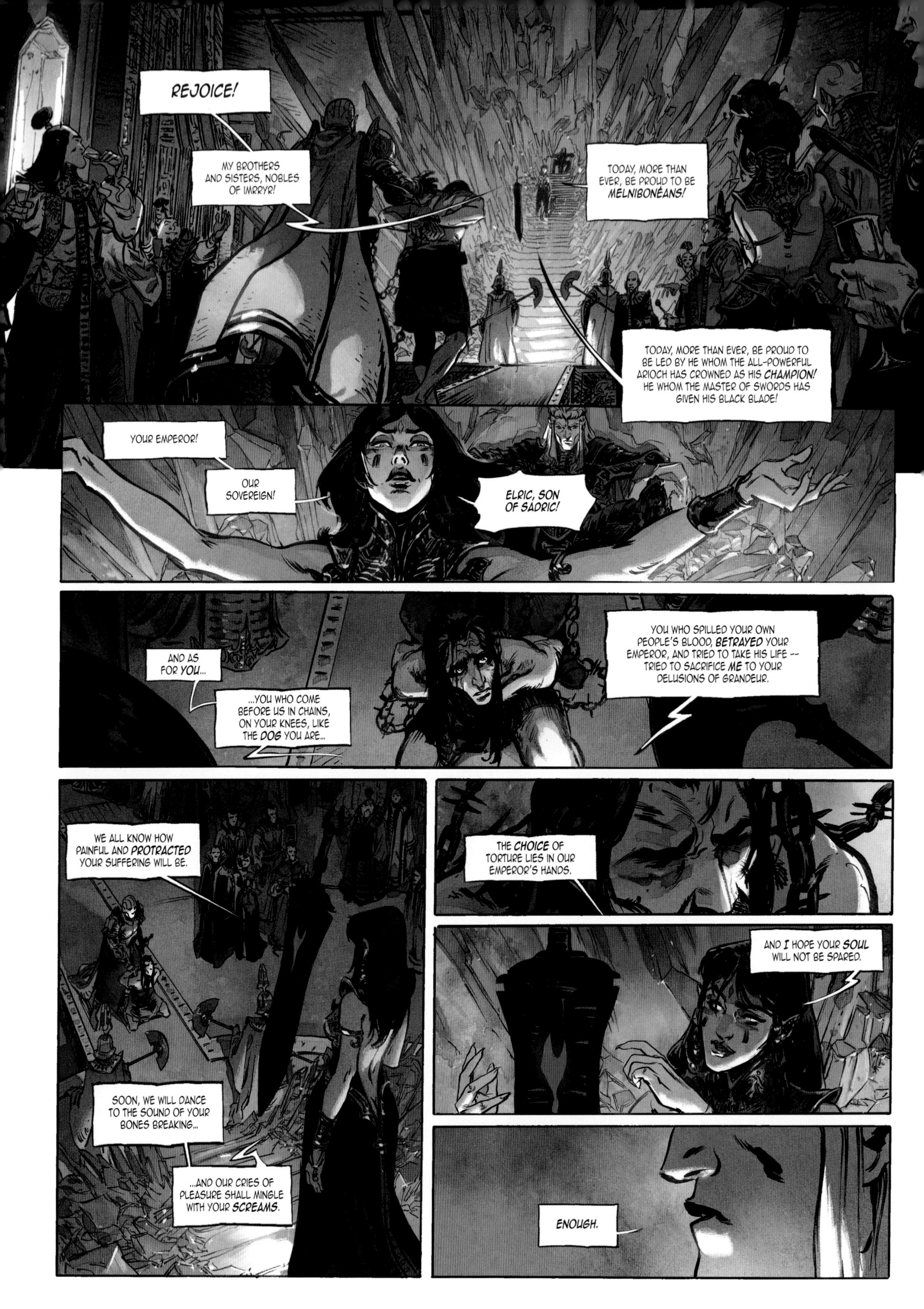
REJOICE!
MY BROTHERS AND SISTERS, NOBLES OF IMRRYR!
TODAY, MORE THAN EVER, BE PROUD TO BE MELNIBONÉANS!
TODAY, MORE THAN EVER, BE PROUD TO BE LED BY HE WHOM THE ALL-POWERFUL ARIOCH HAS CROWNED AS HIS CHAMPION! HE WHOM THE MASTER OF SWORDS HAS GIVEN HIS BLACK BLADE!
YOUR EMPEROR!
OUR SOVEREIGN!
ELRIC, SON OF SADRIC!
AND AS FOR YOU...
...YOU WHO COME BEFORE US IN CHAINS, ON YOUR KNEES, LIKE THE DOG YOU ARE...
YOU WHO SPILLED YOUR OWN PEOPLE'S BLOOD, BETRAYED YOUR EMPEROR, AND TRIED TO TAKE HIS LIFE -- TRIED TO SACRIFICE ME TO YOUR DELUSIONS OF GRANDEUR.
WE ALL KNOW HOW PAINFUL AND PROTRACTED YOUR SUFFERING WILL BE.
SOON, WE WILL DANCE TO THE SOUND OF YOUR BONES BREAKING...
...AND OUR CRIES OF PLEASURE SHALL MINGLE WITH YOUR SCREAMS.
THE CHOICE OF TORTURE LIES IN OUR EMPEROR'S HANDS.
AND I HOPE YOUR SOUL WILL NOT BE SPARED.
ENOUGH.

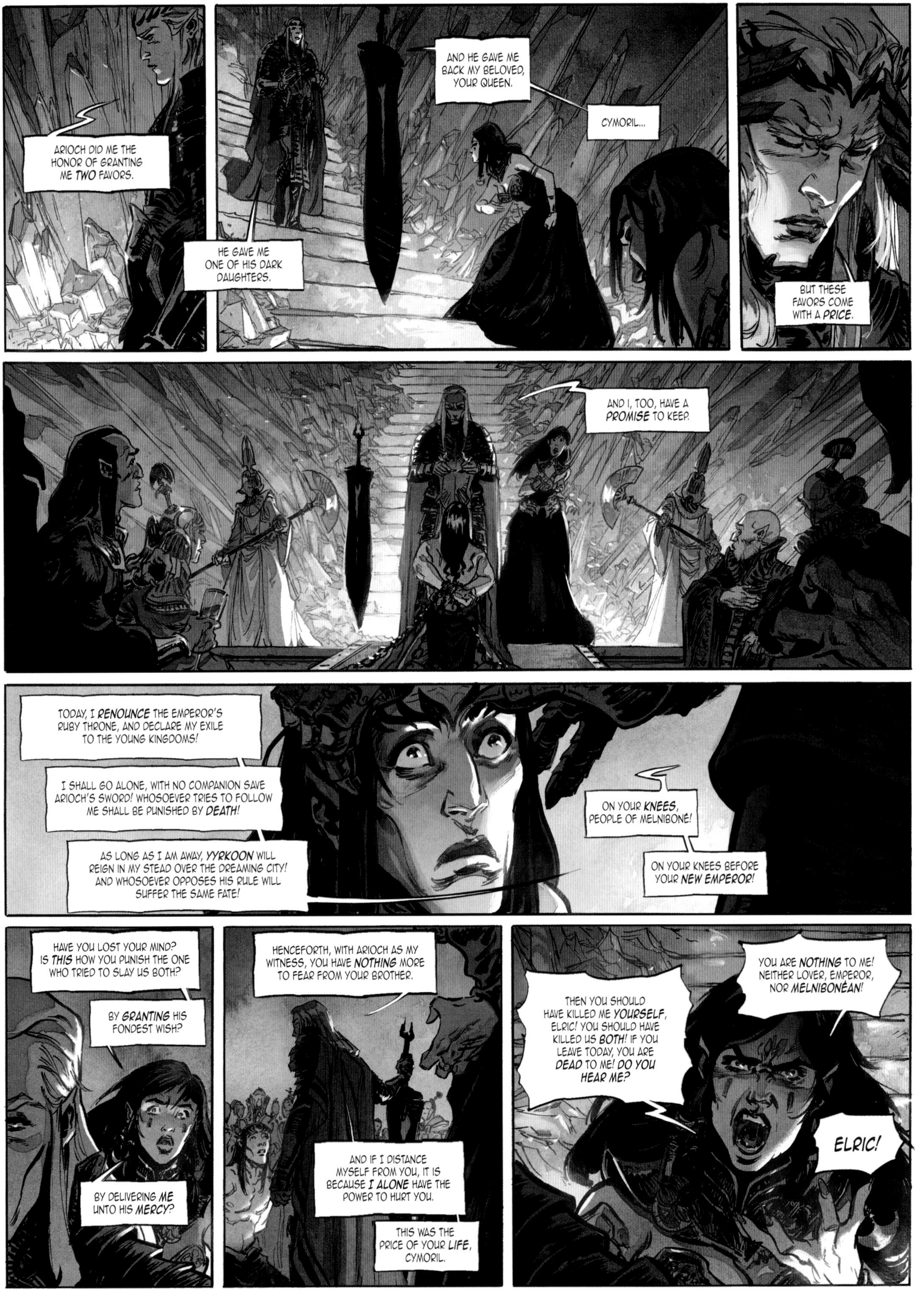
ARIOCH DID ME THE HONOR OF GRANTING ME TWO FAVORS.
HE GAVE ME ONE OF HIS DARK DAUGHTERS.
AND HE GAVE ME BACK MY BELOVED, YOUR QUEEN.
CYMORIL...
BUT THESE FAVORS COME WITH A PRICE.
AND I, TOO, HAVE A PROMISE TO KEEP.
TODAY, I RENOUNCE THE EMPEROR'S RUBY THRONE, AND DECLARE MY EXILE TO THE YOUNG KINGDOMS!
I SHALL GO ALONE, WITH NO COMPANION SAVE ARIOCH'S SWORD! WHOSOEVER TRIES TO FOLLOW ME SHALL BE PUNISHED BY DEATH!
AS LONG AS I AM AWAY, YYRKOON WILL REIGN IN MY STEAD OVER THE DREAMING CITY! AND WHOSOEVER OPPOSES HIS RULE WILL SUFFER THE SAME FATE!
ON YOUR KNEES, PEOPLE OF MELNIBONÉ!
ON YOUR KNEES BEFORE YOUR NEW EMPEROR!
HAVE YOU LOST YOUR MIND? IS THIS HOW YOU PUNISH THE ONE WHO TRIED TO SLAY US BOTH?
BY GRANTING HIS FONDEST WISH?
BY DELIVERING ME UNTO HIS MERCY?
HENCEFORTH, WITH ARIOCH AS MY WITNESS, YOU HAVE NOTHING MORE TO FEAR FROM YOUR BROTHER.
AND IF I DISTANCE MYSELF FROM YOU, IT IS BECAUSE I ALONE HAVE THE POWER TO HURT YOU.
THIS WAS THE PRICE OF YOUR LIFE, CYMORIL.
THEN YOU SHOULD HAVE KILLED ME YOURSELF, ELRIC! YOU SHOULD HAVE KILLED US BOTH! IF YOU LEAVE TODAY, YOU ARE DEAD TO ME! DO YOU HEAR ME?
YOU ARE NOTHING TO ME! NEITHER LOVER, EMPEROR, NOR MELNIBONÉAN!
ELRIC!

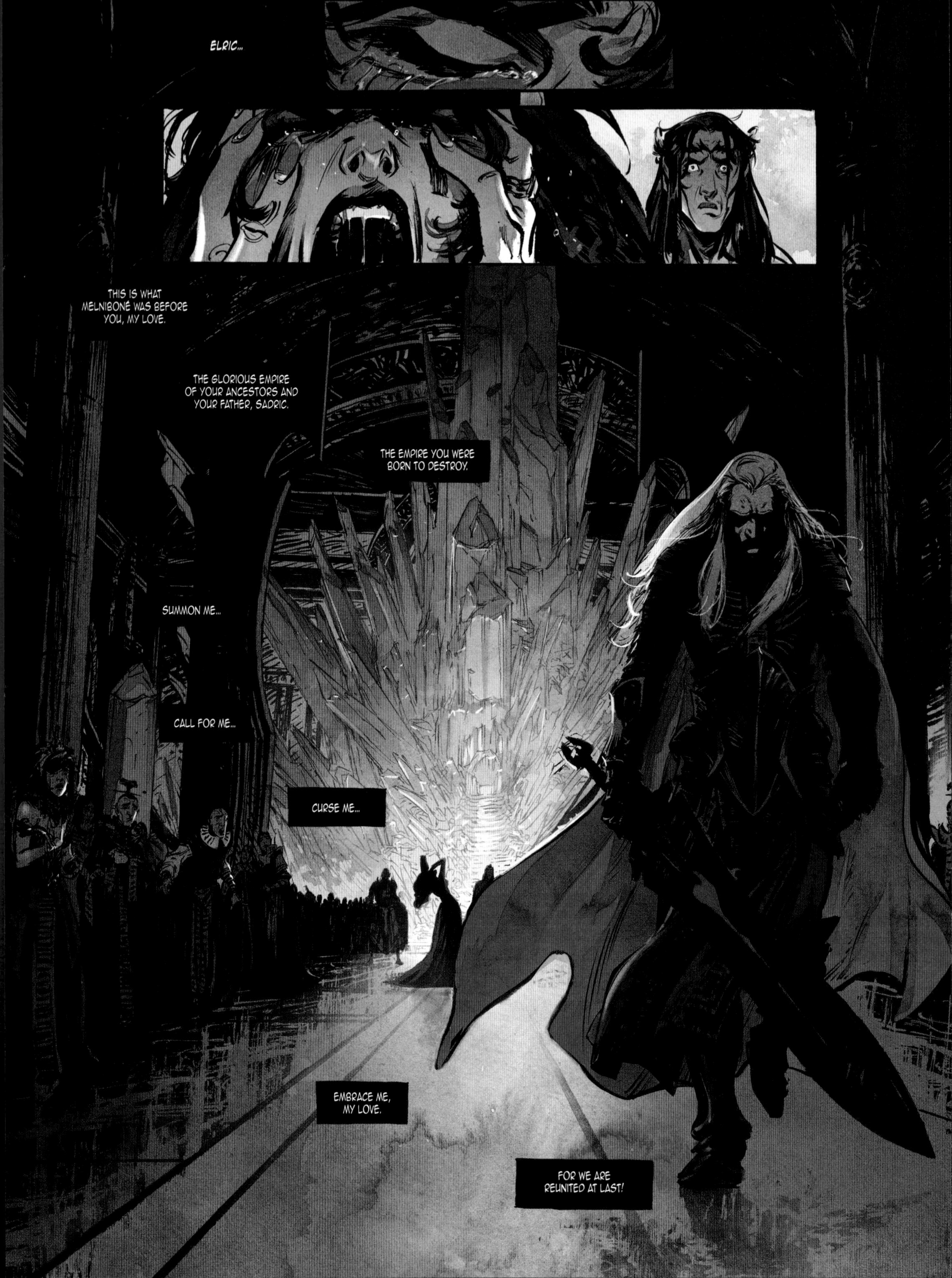
ELRIC...
THIS IS WHAT MELNIBONÉ WAS BEFORE YOU, MY LOVE.
THE GLORIOUS EMPIRE OF YOUR ANCESTORS AND YOUR FATHER, SADRIC.
THE EMPIRE YOU WERE BORN TO DESTROY.
SUMMON ME...
CALL FOR ME...
CURSE ME...
EMBRACE ME, MY LOVE.
FOR WE ARE REUNITED AT LAST!

AUTHORS' BIOS

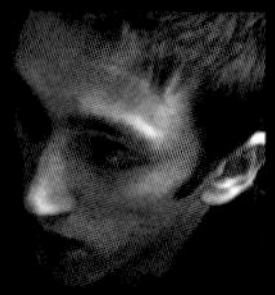

Julien Blondel is a comic book writer, game author and journalist who has had a varied career – including hosting a radio show for nearly 14 years – before becoming a DJ. In 1994, he abandoned the electronica scene for a career in writing. Since then, he has written numerous successful screenplays, comics, games and short stories.

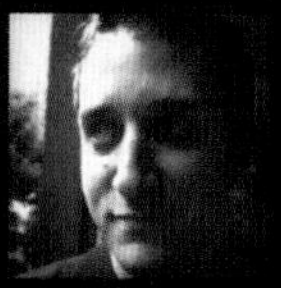

Jean-Luc Cano is a writer and director who has worked for more than ten years in television, film, comics, animation and gaming. Today, he is working on several projects, including the completion of his first feature film.

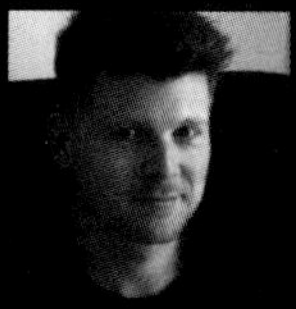

Julien Telo is passionate about comics, animation, and illustration. He studied graphic design at the University of Blois, and there published some of his first work with the collective, 'Café Salé'. In 2010, he joined the Elyum Studio, where he met Didier Poli and Robin Recht.

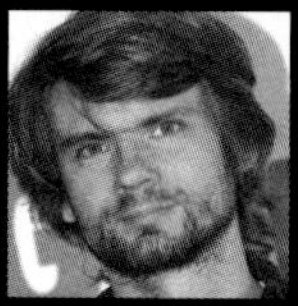

Robin Recht has illustrated *DmC: Devil May Cry*, the dark romance series *Totendom*, and a prequel title to the *Third Testament* series, the *Julius* trilogy.

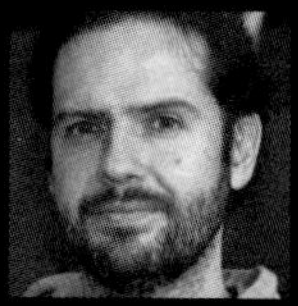

Didier Poli has worked for various animation studios, including Disney studios on *Tarzan*, and as the Art Director for Kalisto Entertainment. As well as working in comics, he is a sought-after designer and storyboard artist for animated movies and games.

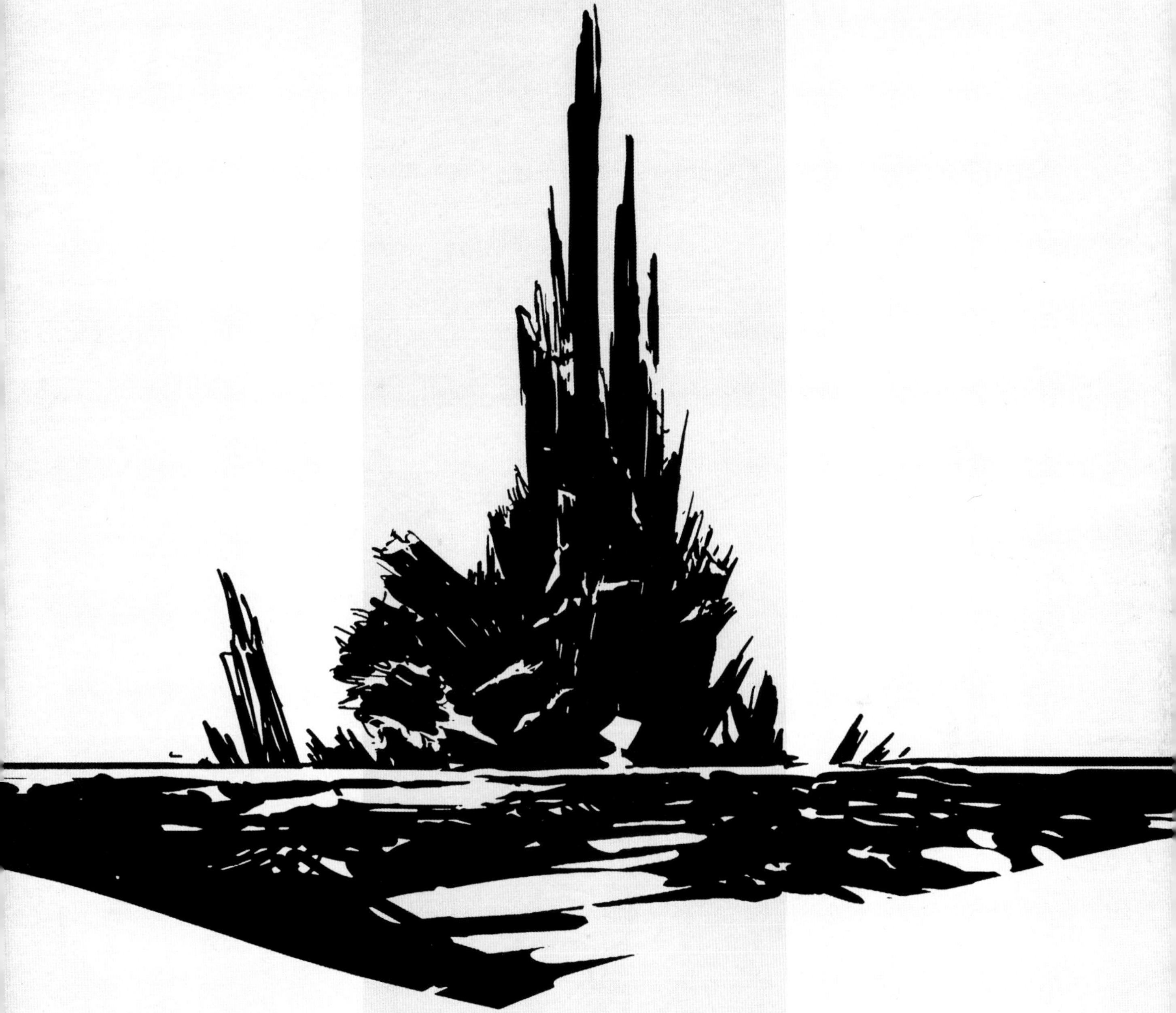

GENESIS

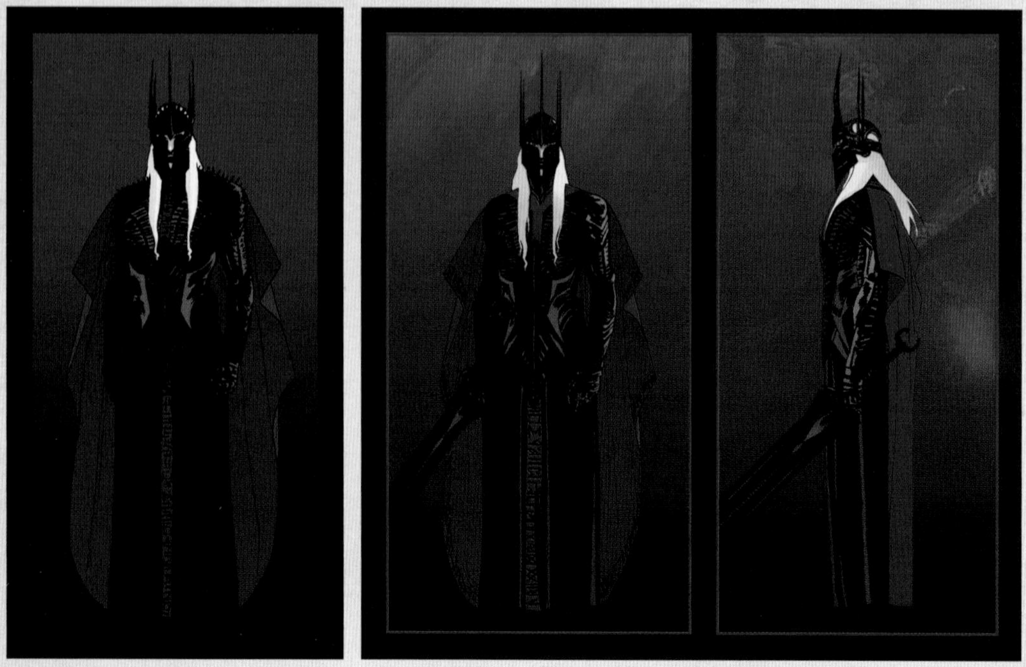
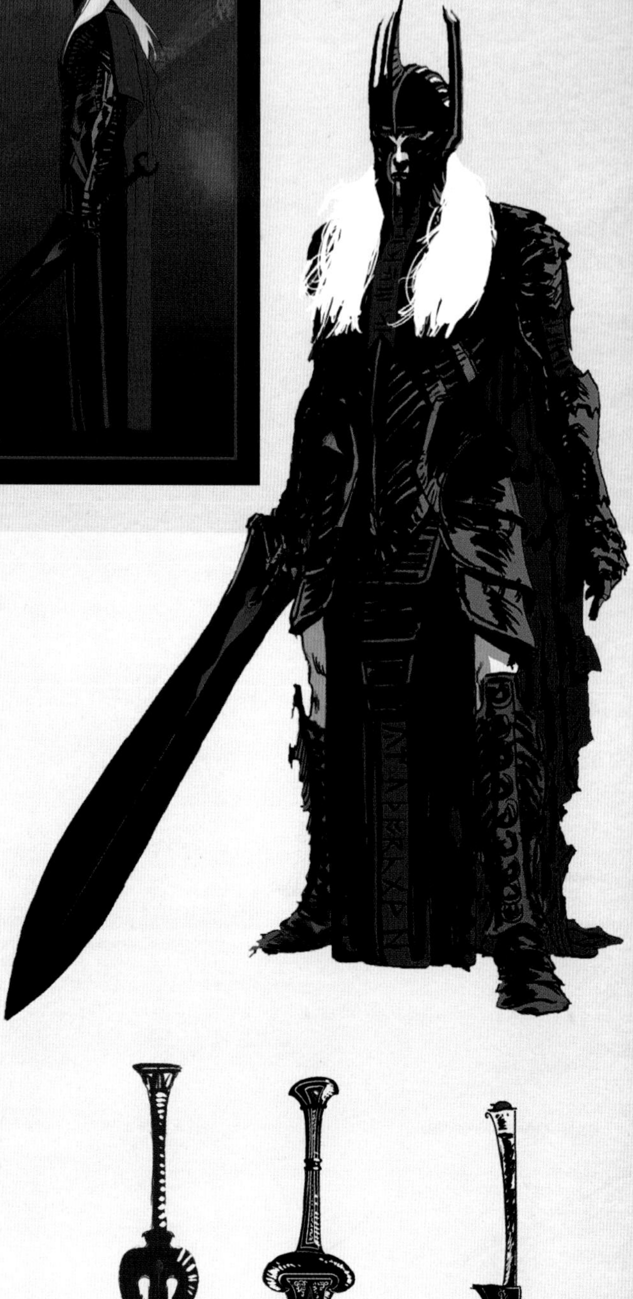
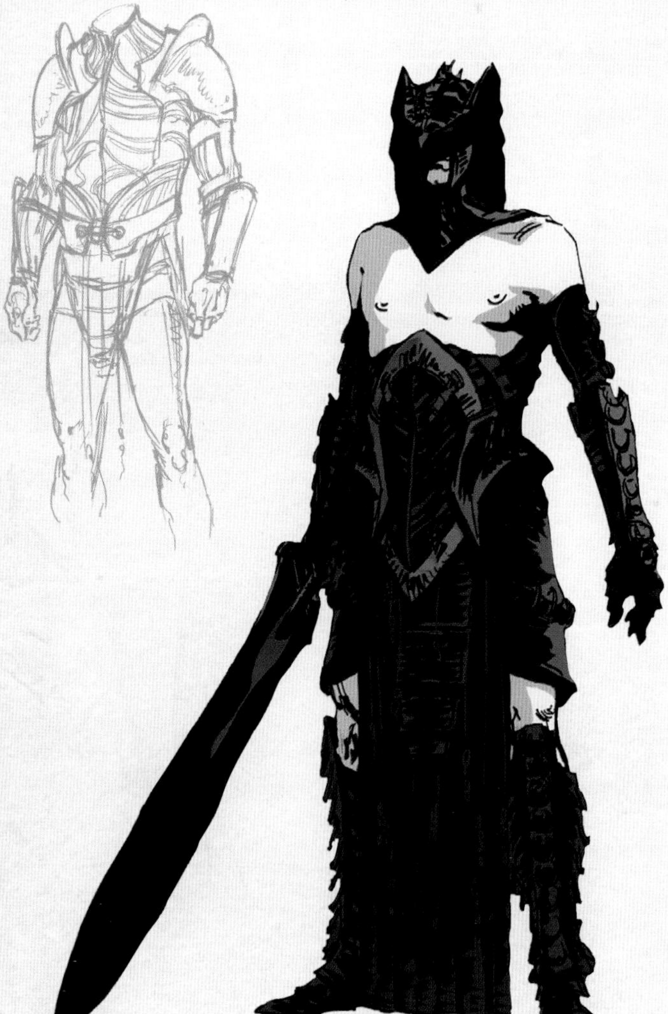
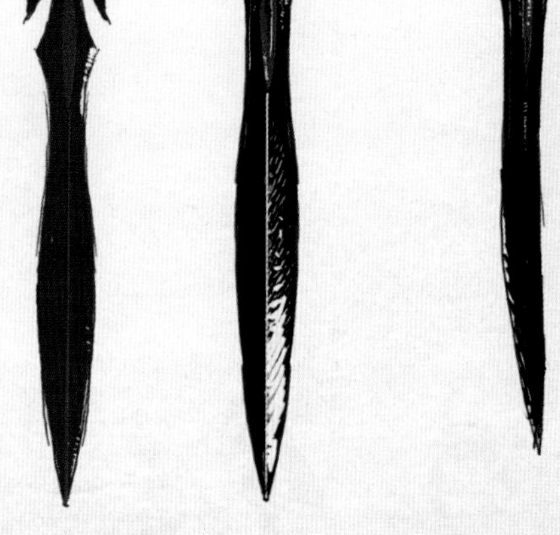

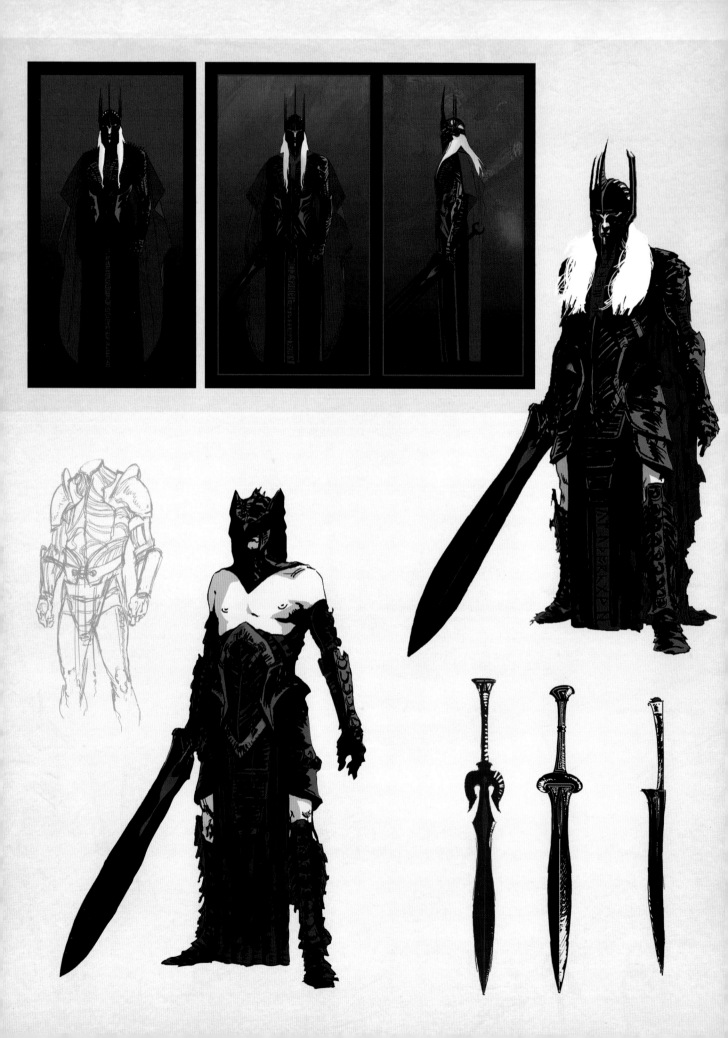

ELRIC AND STORMBRINGER

Studies for Elric in different outfits (official, combat, travel), and for Stormbringer, the sword soon to be his constant companion, thanks to Arioch's machinations. The beginning of the relationship between Elric and his weapon form the heart of Book II.

THE DRAGON CAVES

Fulfilling a sacred and hereditary duty, Dyvim Tvar is Lord of the Dragon Caves, a place as dangerous as it is emblematic of Melniboné. An ideal setting for the creators to begin sketching the most representative creatures of all fantasy, even if they don't yet appear in this story.

NEW TALENTS

For Book II, a new artistic team was formed, but their goal remained the same as for the first book: a blending of skills and talents leading to a collaborative work whose every page was more than the sum of what its contributors provided. To begin with, there was the work of literary adaptation, which fell to Julien Bondel and Jean-Luc Cano, each bouncing off the other's suggestions. Then came the storyboarding phase, the skeleton of the page to come, which Julien Blondel and Robin Recht tackled in a back-and-forth process of constant adjustments. After that came the pencils, which Julien Telo brought to life, and then inks, which Robin Recht handled. Once the page was turned into a digital file, Julien Telo went back over it to make corrections as needed in digital post-production, even if that meant completely re-drawing certain panels from scratch with Robin Recht. Finally came the coloring process, overseen by Scarlett Smulkowski, with help from Robin Recht and Jean Bastide in the final stages. As the following example shows, the conception and maturation of each page follows a long, eventful path full of transformations.

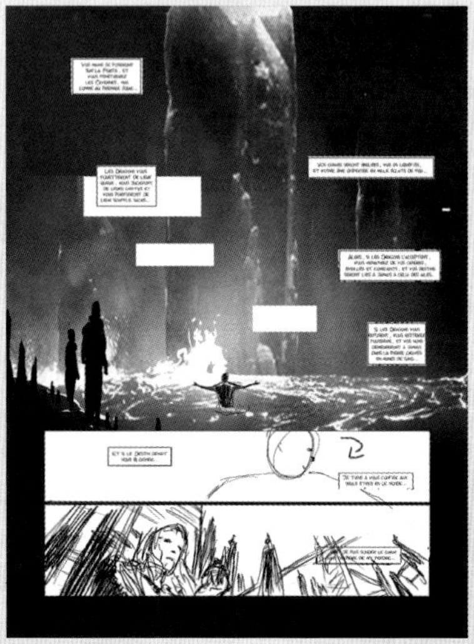
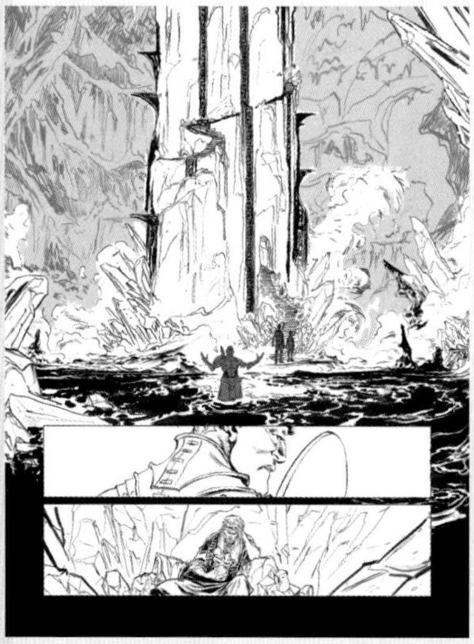
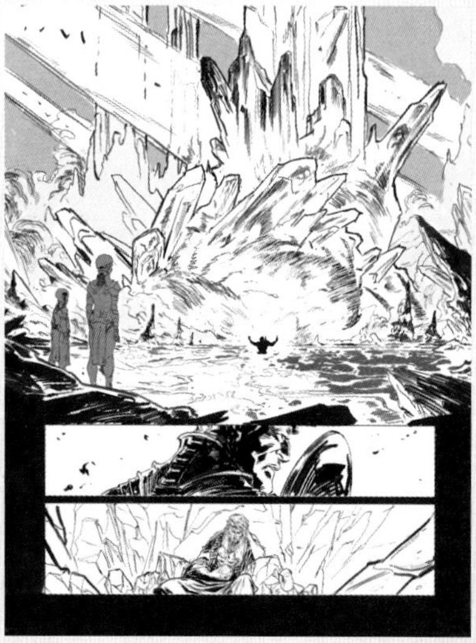
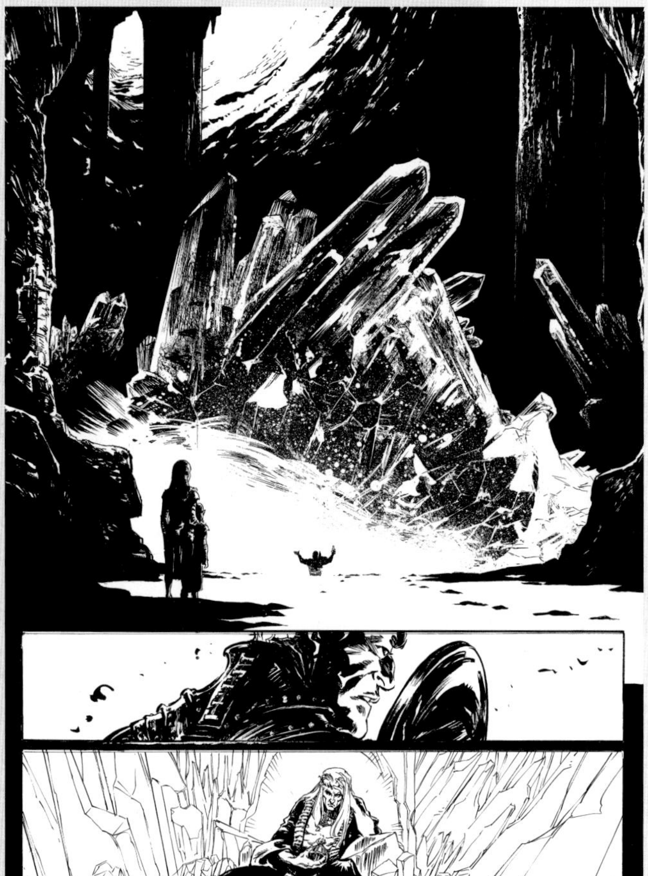
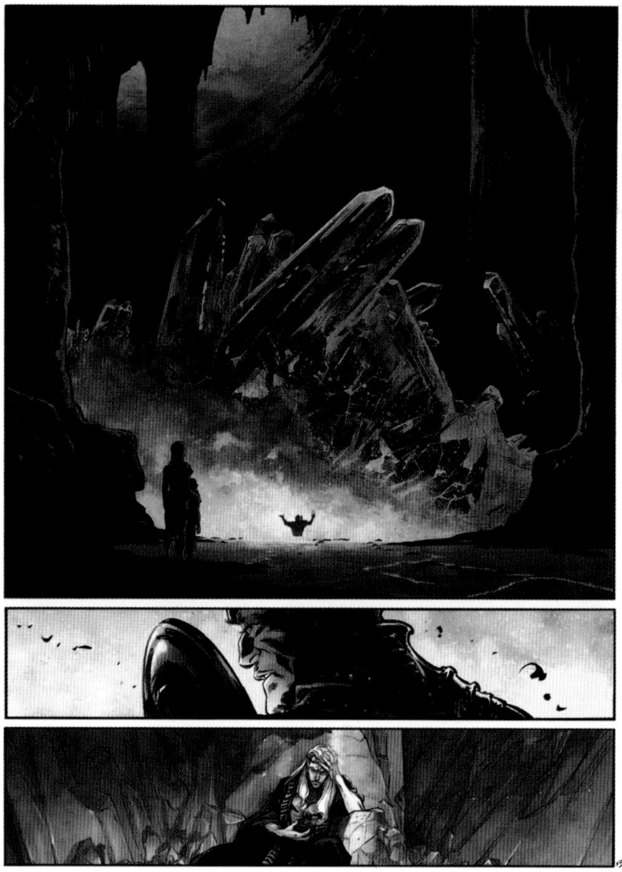

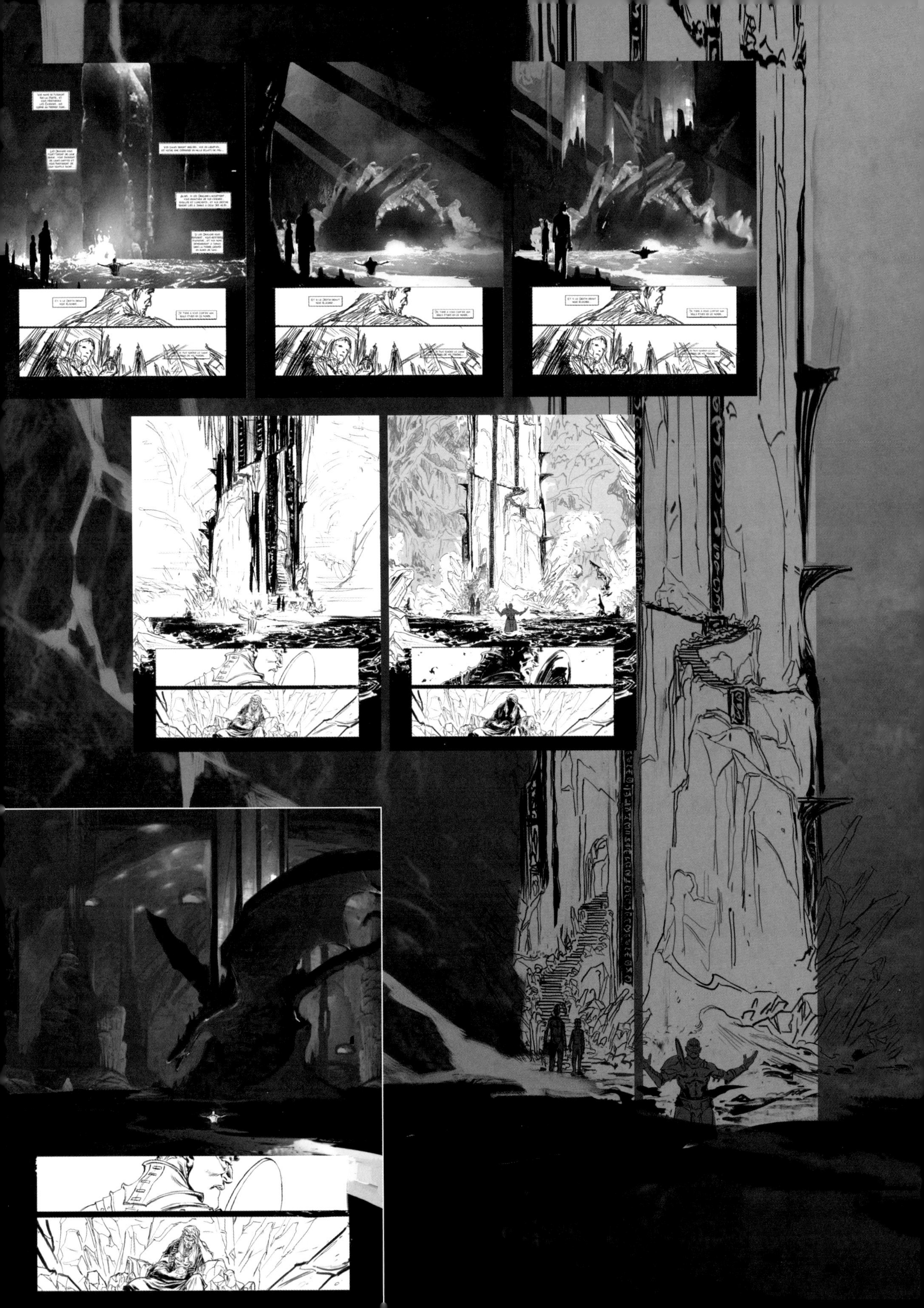

THE MICHAEL MOORCOCK COLLECTION: FICTION

THE ETERNAL CHAMPION

Reborn to save humanity, the Eternal Champion battles the timeless enemies of Earth.

"THE MOST IMPORTANT SUCCESSOR TO MERVYN PEAKE AND WYNDHAM LEWIS"
J.G. BALLARD
MICHAEL MOORCOCK
THE ETERNAL CHAMPION
THE ETERNAL CHAMPION SEQUENCE
BOOK ONE

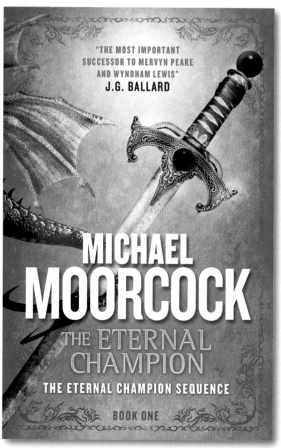

ISBN: 9781783291618

"THE MOST IMPORTANT SUCCESSOR TO MERVYN PEAKE AND WYNDHAM LEWIS"
J.G. BALLARD
MICHAEL MOORCOCK
PHOENIX IN OBSIDIAN
THE ETERNAL CHAMPION SEQUENCE
BOOK TWO

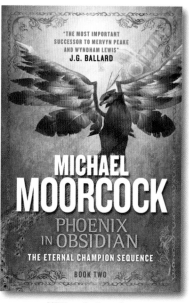

ISBN: 9781783291625

"THE MOST IMPORTANT SUCCESSOR TO MERVYN PEAKE AND WYNDHAM LEWIS"
J.G. BALLARD
MICHAEL MOORCOCK
THE DRAGON IN THE SWORD
THE ETERNAL CHAMPION SEQUENCE
BOOK THREE

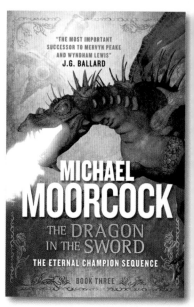

ISBN: 9781783291632

A NOMAD OF THE TIME STREAMS

"The greatest writer of post-Tolkien British fantasy"
MICHAEL CHABON
MICHAEL MOORCOCK
THE WARLORD OF THE AIR
A NOMAD OF THE TIME STREAMS NOVEL 1

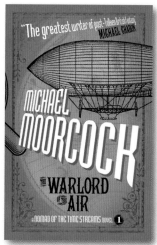

ISBN: 9781781161456

THE LAND LEVIATHAN
MICHAEL MOORCOCK
"The greatest writer of post-Tolkien British fantasy"
MICHAEL CHABON
A NOMAD OF THE TIME STREAMS NOVEL 2

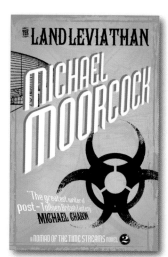

ISBN: 9781781161463

"The greatest writer of post-Tolkien British fantasy"
MICHAEL CHABON
STEEL TSAR
MICHAEL MOORCOCK
A NOMAD OF THE TIME STREAMS NOVEL 3

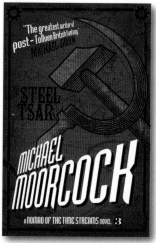

ISBN: 9781781161470

Also available... THE CHRONICLES OF CORUM: *The Knight of the Swords* (May 2015), *The Queen of the Swords* (June 2015), *The King of the Swords* (July 2015), *The Bull and the Spear* (August 2015), *The Oak and the Ram* (September 2015), *The Sword and the Stallion* (October 2015). THE CORNELIUS QUARTET: *The Final Programme* (February 2016)*A Cure for Cancer* (March 2016), *The English Assassin* (April 2016), *The Condition of Muzak* (May 2016)

TITANBOOKS.COM

THE MICHAEL MOORCOCK COLLECTION: COMICS

MICHAEL MOORCOCK
ELRIC
THE RUBY THRONE
BLONDEL · POLI · RECHT · BASTIDE

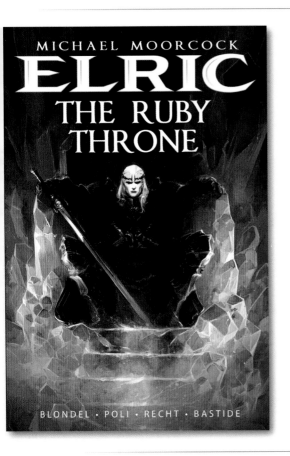

ELRIC: THE RUBY THRONE

ISBN: 978-1782760931

Seated on the Ruby Throne, looking down upon the opulence and bloody majesty of Melniboné, is the melancholy albino emperor, Elric. Plaything of the Lords of Chaos, threatened by intrigue from within his own palace and destined to bring about the ruin of his own people!

TO ME, MELNIBONÉ!

THE CLASSIC COMICS

THE MICHAEL MOORCOCK LIBRARY
Elric
OF MELNIBONÉ
ROY THOMAS
MICHAEL T. GILBERT
P.CRAIG RUSSEL

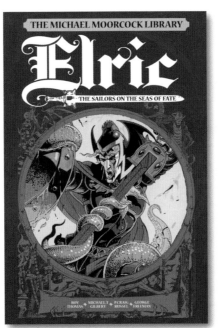

ELRIC OF MELNIBONÉ

ISBN: 978-1782762881

On sale 03/24/2015

THE MICHAEL MOORCOCK LIBRARY
Elric
THE SAILORS ON THE SEAS OF FATE

ELRIC: THE SAILORS ON THE SEAS OF FATE

ISBN: 978-1782762898

On sale 06/23/2015

THE MICHAEL MOORCOCK LIBRARY
Elric
WEIRD OF THE WHITE WOLF

ELRIC: WEIRD OF THE WHITE WOLF

ISBN: 978-1782762904

On sale 09/29/2015

TITANCOMICS.COM

ALSO FROM TITAN COMICS

MICHAEL MOORCOCK
ELRIC
THE RUBY THRONE
BLONDEL • POLI • RECHT • BASTIDE

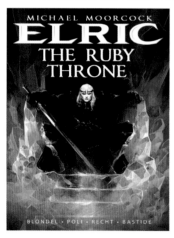

ELRIC
THE RUBY THRONE
ISBN: 978-1782760931

THE GRAPHIC NOVEL THAT INSPIRED THE FILM
SNOW
PIERCER
1: THE ESCAPE
LOB • ROCHETTE

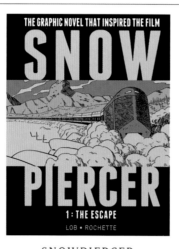

SNOWPIERCER
VOL. 1: THE ESCAPE
ISBN: 978-1782761334

THE GRAPHIC NOVEL THAT INSPIRED THE FILM
SNOW
2
PIERCER
2: THE EXPLORERS
LEGRAND • ROCHETTE

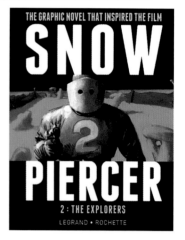

SNOWPIERCER
VOL. 2: THE EXPLORERS
ISBN: 978-1782761365

LEHMAN / CRÉTY
MASKED
ANOMALIES

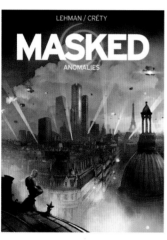

MASKED:
ANOMALIES
ISBN: 978-1782761082

WORLD
WAR
X
BOOK
1
JERRY FRISSEN / PETER SNEJBJERG

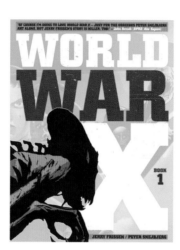

WORLD WAR X:
HELIUS
ISBN: 978-1782761129

THE
CHIMERA
BRIGADE
LEHMAN
COLIN
GESS
BESSONNEAU

THE CHIMERA BRIGADE:
VOLUME 1
ISBN: 978-1782760993

ROYAL
BLOOD
"SIMPLY
SUPERB"
JODOROWSKY • LIU

ROYAL BLOOD
ISBN: 978-1782760979

THE THIRD
TESTAMENT
BOOK 1:
THE LION AWAKES
"ONE OF THE BEST
SERIES OF THE
PAST DECADE"
ALEX ALICE ✣ XAVIER DORISON

THE THIRD TESTAMENT:
THE LION AWAKES
ISBN: 978-1782760894

THE CHRONICLES OF
LEGION
THE
THREE
LIVES OF
DRACULA

THE CHRONICLES
OF LEGION
ISBN: 978-1782760931

FOR MORE INFORMATION VISIT **titan-comics.com**

facebook.com/comicstitan @ComicsTitan

Jharkor

Shazaar

STRAIT OF CHAOS

Pan Tang

YOUNG KINGDOMS

THE DRAGON SEA

SORCERERS ISLE

Melniboné

BOILING SEA